Complete Modern Chinese Grammar

Intermediate to Advanced

INTERNATIONAL
FOREIGN LANGUAGE
ASSOCIATE PRESS

Paul Christian Brown

Complete Modern Chinese Grammar - Intermediate to Advanced

Author's name: Paul Christian Brown

Publisher: International Foreign Language Associate Press, Canterbury.

ISBN: 978-1-909601-06-2

Printed and bound by Lightning Source UK Ltd, Milton Keynes, UK

Contents

Contents

Contents

Contents

Contents

Contents

I would like to thank my teachers at Wenzhou University, China

for inspiring me and others to continue

with our studies and finish what we started.

Reference:

Murphy M., English Grammar in Use. *A self-study reference and practice book for intermediate leaners of English*. 4th Ed. Cambridge University Press. 2012

Pasden. J., *Chinese Grammar Wiki Book (Elementary)*. Allset Learning. 2017.

Pasden J., *Chinese Grammar Wiki Book (Intermediate)*. Allset Learning. 2017.

Ross, C & Jing-Heng, S. M., *Modern Mandarin Chinese Grammar: A practical guide*. 2nd Ed. London & New York. Routledge. 2014.

Chinese converter 2012-2019, Chinese Converter. Viewed 01 Feb - 5 June 2020,

<https://www.chineseconverter.com/en/convert/chinese-to-pinyin>

Pin1yin1 2020, Pinyin Converter, Viewed 01 Feb-31 May 2020,

<https://www.pin1yin1.com/>

Chinese boost 2020, Chinese Boost, Viewed 03 & 21 April, 21 & 19 May 2020, <https://www.chineseboost.com/>

Google Fonts. 2020. Google fonts. Viewed 8 January, 2020.

<https://www.fonts.google.com>

Paul Christian Brown

A word from the author:

Having spent years trying to learn Mandarin the traditional way, I quickly realised that the logic behind it was not suitable for me. Therefore, as a teacher I have spent the last 5 years designing a Chinese grammar book which allows a native-born English speaker to go from English grammar to Mandarin, rather than the traditional way of starting from Chinese grammar and then relating it to English grammar. In this way, a native-English speaker, who thinks in English, can learn to translate from English to Mandarin using this style of learning.

Who is this book for?

This book is for anyone wishing to learn how to use Chinese for speaking, reading and writing. The information contained within beginner to intermediate and intermediate to advanced is enough to pass HSK 5, but the books themselves are designed to get non-native speakers to actually use Mandarin on a day-to-day basis. You might want to send messages, write emails, conduct in-depth conversations, or give presentations in Mandarin. If so, then the intermediate to advanced edition provides all the grammar needed to communicate with native Chinese people about any issue, from everyday to more serious and specific.

How to use the book:

The book is divided into 140 units, and after every 7 units there is a summary page that can be used to review what has been studied. With this book, students can add depth and weight to their spoken and written Mandarin. If students do not have a basic grasp of Chinese grammar, then the beginner to intermediate edition is recommended before commencement of this book.

By the end of this book, students should be able to talk and write to an intermediate and advanced level. Students will certainly be able to sit HSK 5 test and feel confident of passing.

Here is the word order for different types of sentences that are used on a regular basis:

(Subject + verb + direct object)

I drink green tea.

我喝绿茶。Wǒ hē lǜchá.

(Subject + verb + indirect object + direct object)

I give money to her.

我给她钱。Wǒ gěi tā qián.

(Subject + location + verb)

I eat at home.

我在家里吃饭。Tā zài jiā lǐ chīfàn.

(Subject + prepositional phrase + verb)

Sara drinks coffee with me.

萨拉跟我一起喝咖啡。Sàlā gēn wǒ yīqǐ hē kāfēi.

(Subject + prepositional phrase + indirect object + direct object)

I give a present to my mother with my father.

我跟我爸爸给妈妈很多礼物。Wǒ gēn wǒ bàba gěi māma hěn duō lǐwù.

(Subject + time/when + prepositional phrase + verb)

I play with some friends every day.

我每天跟一些朋友玩。Wǒ měi tiān gēn yīxiē péngyǒu wán.

(Subject + time/when + adverb + verb)

Peter always watches television at night on Wednesday.

皮特在周三晚上总是看电视。Pítè zài zhōusān wǎnshàng zǒngshì kàn diànshì.

(Subject + time/when + location + verb (phrase）

I have a meeting in my office at 9:00 a.m. every day.

我每天早上九点钟在办公室里有会议。

Wǒ měi tiān zǎoshàng jiǔ diǎn zhōng zài bàngōngshì lǐ yǒu huìyì.

Here is the word order for different types of sentences that are used on a regular basis:

(Subject + adverb + prepositional phrase + verb)

He definitely goes out with his wife to eat.

他肯定跟他妻子一起出去吃。 Tā kěndìng gēn tā qīzi yīqǐ chūqù chī.

(Subject + time/when + location + prepositional phrase + verb or verb phrase)

I play poker with my mother at home every Monday.

我每个周一在家里跟我妈妈一起打扑克。 Wǒ měi gè zhōuyī zài jiā lǐ gēn wǒ māma yīqǐ dǎ pūkè.

Duration always goes at the end of a sentence:

I lived in Beijing for 3 years. 我在北京住了三年。 Wǒ zài Běijīng zhù le sān nián.

Negation (不) for present tense and (没) for past tense. They go before verb:

I don't like drinking alcohol. 我**不**喜欢喝酒精。 Wǒ bù xǐhuān hē jiǔjīng.

She doesn't have any money. 她**没**有钱。 Tā méi yǒu qián.

He didn't come last night. 他昨晚**没**来。 Tā zuówǎn méi lái.

Placement of aspect particles (着，了，过):

I am washing clothes. 我在洗**着**衣服。 Wǒ zài xǐzhe yīfú.

I washed clothes last night. 我昨天晚上洗衣服**了**。 Wǒ zuótiān wǎnshàng xǐ yīfú le.

I once washed clothes. 我曾经洗**过**衣服。 Wǒ céngjīng xǐguò yīfú.

It is used when talking about actions that occur quickly, not actions that have previously been arranged. It is also used for lifting things in an upward movement and for specific verbs:

to stand up 站起来 zhànqǐlái   to remember 想起来 xiǎngqǐlái

to hold up 举起来 jǔqǐlái   to think of 想起来 xiǎngqǐlái

It is used with (把) sentences:

I held up my bookcase. 我把我的书架举起来了。Wǒ bǎ wǒ de shūjià jǔqǐlái le.

I have to **put my** clothes **away** when I get home.

当我回家的时候，我不得不**把**衣服收**起来**。Dāng wǒ huíjiā de shíhòu, wǒ bùdé bù bǎ yīfú

shōuqǐlái.

It can also be used to say that a certain action has already begun and is still happening now:

All the lions started **fighting** each other.

所有的狮子互相交战**起来**了。Suǒyǒu de shīzi hùxiāng jiāozhànqǐlái le.

After we went outside, the weather started **getting** colder.

我们出去以后，天气开始冷**起来**了。Wǒmen chūqù yǐhòu, tiānqì kāishǐ lěngqǐlái le.

It is also used to talk about abstract concepts such as bringing things together:

If we work **together**, (then) we can complete it on time.

如果我们一起工作**起来**，**就**有可能准时完成。

Rúguǒ wǒmen yīqǐ gōngzuòqǐlái, jiù yǒu kěnéng zhǔnshí wánchéng.

If we can **join** our company with theirs, (then) we could become the best in the world.

如果我们公司和他们的公司联合**起来**，**就**有可能成为世界上最好的公司。

Rúguǒ wǒmen gōngsī hé tāmen gōngsī liánhéqǐlái, jiù yǒu kěnéng chéngwèi shìjiè shàng

zùihǎo de gōngsī.

For some rhetorical questions, the (呢) is used as follows:

I think this is very good. What about you?

我认为这是很好的，你觉得**呢**？ Wǒ rènwéi zhè shì hěn hǎo de, nǐ juéde ne?

These are nice. What about those?

这些是好的，那些**呢**？ Zhèxiē shì hǎo de, nàxiē ne?

My father is a carpenter. What about your father?

我爸爸是一名木工，你爸爸**呢**？ Wǒ bàba shì yī míng mùgōng, nǐ bàba ne?

When making a guess or to show that you have some doubt (莫非) is used:

Could he be a reliable person?

莫非他真的是一个可靠的人？ Mòfēi tā zhēn de shì yī gè kěkào de rén?

Could it be that she forgot to phone her?

莫非她真的忘记打电话给她？ Mòfēi tā zhēn de wàngjì dǎ diànhuà gěi tā?

(难道) is also used at the beginning of a statement to form a rhetorical question. Add (什么)

after verb or between separable verbs as normal:

You are not saying that you cannot meet me tonight?

难道你是说你今晚不可能见我吗？ Nándào nǐ shì shuō nǐ jīnwǎn bù kěnéng jiàn wǒ ma?

You are telling me that you believe this is an appropriate solution?

难道你相信这是一个合适的结果吗？ Nándào nǐ xiāngxìn zhè shì yī gè héshì de jiéguǒ ma?

You're telling me that you didn't know that he was my brother?

难道你不是在说你不知道他是我的哥哥吗？ Nándào nǐ bú shì zài shuō nǐ bù zhīdào tā shì wǒ de gēge ma?

You might want to confirm something with somebody. To emphasise confirmation, you can add (吗) to a question that already has an interrogative pronoun:

What is this?

这是什么？ Zhè shì shénme?

Do you know what this is?

你知道这是什么吗？ Nǐ zhīdào zhè shì shénme ma?

Where does she live?

她住在哪里？ Tā zhù zài nǎlǐ?

Do you know where she lives?

你知道她住在哪里吗？ Nǐ zhīdào tā zhù zài nǎlǐ ma?

Whose money is it?

这是谁的钱？ Zhè shì shéi de qián?

Do you know whose money this is?

你知道这钱是谁的吗？ Nǐ zhīdào zhè qián shì shéi de ma?

Who are those people over there?

那边的人是谁？ Nàbiān de rén shì shéi?

Do you know who those people over there are?

你知道那边的人是谁吗？ Nǐ zhīdào nàbiān de rén shì shéi ma?

Why isn't he going?

他为什么不去？ Tā wèi shénme bú qù?

Do you know why he isn't going?

你知道为什么他不去吗？ Nǐ zhīdào wèi shénme tā bú qù ma?

In Mandarin, there are six verbs that often cause problems because their meanings can be similar:

知道 zhīdào   理解 lǐjiě

了解 liǎojiě   认识 rènshi

懂 dǒng   明白 míngbái

These six words all mean 'to know'

but their usage is often different.

(知道) to know something about something or somebody in a general sense:

I **know** (something about) Hilary Clinton. 我**知道**希拉里：克林顿。 Wǒ zhīdào Xīlālǐ: Kèlíndùn.

I **know** what it is. 我**知道**它是什么。 Wǒ zhīdào tā shì shénme.

I **know** how to do it. 我**知道**该怎么做。Wǒ zhīdào gāi zěnme zuò.

(理解) to know or make sense of something in greater detail:

He **could understand** that story. 他能**理解**那个故事。Tā néng lǐjiě nà gè gùshì.

Bob **cannot understand** my ideas. 鲍勃**无法理解**我的看法。Bàobó wúfǎ lǐjiě wǒ de kànfǎ.

Tim **couldn't grasp** the issue. 蒂姆**无法理解**这道难题。Dìmǔ wúfǎ lǐjiě zhè dào nántí.

(了解) to come to know or understand something about somebody or something:

I **don't understand** much about her yet. 我还**不够了解**她。Wǒ hái bú gòu liáojiě tā.

I **know** a lot about his artwork. 关于他的艺术品我**了解**很多。Guānyú tā de yìshù pǐn wǒ liǎojiě

hěn duō.

(认识) to recognise somebody who you have previously met or seen:

I **know** her. 我**认识**她。Wǒ rènshi tā.

I **know** him from my party. 我从聚会上**认识**他。Wǒ cóng jùhuì shàng rènshi tā.

Here are some more examples related to being able or not being able to understand something:

I **understand** what the teacher said/says.

我**听得懂**老师说的话。   我**明白**老师说的话。

Wǒ tīngdedǒng lǎoshī shuō de huà.   Wǒ míngbái lǎoshī shuō de huà.

I **don't understand** what she is saying.

我**听不懂**她在说什么。   我**不明白**她在说什么。

Wǒ tīngbudǒng tā zài shuō shénme.   Wǒ bù míngbái tā zài shuō shénme.

I **understand** what this passage means.

我**看得懂**这段文章的意思。   我**明白**这段文章的意思。

Wǒ kàndedǒng zhè duàn wénzhāng de yìsi.   Wǒ míngbái zhè duàn wénzhāng de yìsi.

I **don't understand** what this newspaper says.

我**看不懂**这家报纸的内容。   我**不明白**这家报纸的内容。

Wǒ kànbudǒng zhè jiā bàozhǐ de nèiróng.   Wǒ bù míngbái zhè jiā bàozhǐ de nèiróng.

However, (懂) and (明白) are not always used in the same way: (懂) means that a person knows how to do something; (明白) means a person is clear about something that has been read or heard:

She **knows** maths **very well**.   He **really knows** Portuguese.

她**很懂**数学。 Tā hěndǒng shùxué.   他**真的很懂**葡萄牙语。 Tā zhēn de hěndǒng Pútáoyáyǔ.

I **know** her mother.   Eric knows many Chinese characters.

我**了**解她妈妈。 Wǒ liǎojiě tā māma.   埃里克**认识**很多汉字。 Āilǐkè rènshi hěn duō hànzì.

I **understand** what they say.   =   I am **clear** about what they say.

我很**明白**他们说什么。   =   我很**清楚**他们说什么。

Wǒ hěn míngbái tāmen shuō shénme.   Wǒ hěn qīngchǔ tāmen shuō shénme.

When you want to say that you 'used to do something', (曾经...verb + 过) is used:

I **used to** play computer games every day.

我**曾经**每天都**玩过**电脑游戏。Wǒ céngjīng měi tiān dōu wánguò diànniǎo yóuxì.

I **used to go** there with my parents.

我**曾经**跟我父母一起**去过**那里。Wǒ céngjīng gēn wǒ fùmǔ yīqǐ qùguò nàlǐ.

There used to be a post office in the village.

在村里**曾经有**一个邮局。Zài cūn lǐ céngjīng yǒu yī gè yóujú. (No 过 with 有)

There used to be more restaurants in our city.

在我们的城市里**曾经有**比较多的餐馆。Zài wǒmen de chéngshì lǐ céngjīng yǒu bjiào duō de cāiguǎn.

You can also say that something 'used to be' + adjective:

She **used to be** extremely beautiful.

她**曾经**非常漂亮。Tā céngjīng fēicháng piàoliang. (No 过 with adjectives)

Father's cooking **used to be** terrible.

父亲做的饭**曾经**很糟糕。Fùqīn zuò de fàn céngjīng hěn zāogāo.

For things that you 'didn't use to...' either (不曾) or (未曾) can be used:

I **didn't use to** travel during the winter.

我在冬天**不曾**旅行**过**。Wǒ zài dōngtiān bùcéng lǚxíng guò.

She **didn't use to** waste time watching TV.

她**未曾**浪费**过**时间在看电视上。Tā wèicéng làngfèi guò shíjiān zài kàn diànshì shàng.

The previous statements used verbs regarding actions, but when using verbs that state that something 'used to exist' either in a certain place or in a certain condition, then (曾经...是/在/有) are used:

She **used to be** my wife.

她**曾经是**我的太太。Tā céngjīng shì wǒ de tàitai. (No 过 with 是)

I **used to** live next to a police station.

我**曾经**住在警察局旁边。 Wǒ céngjīng zhù zài jǐngchájú pángbiān. (No 过 with 在)

I **used to** have a pet snake.

我**曾经有**一条宠物蛇。Wǒ céngjīng yǒu yī tiáo chǒngwù shé. (No 过 with 有)

Since the questions are yes/no types, just add (吗) to the statement:

Did you **use to** go to school on foot?

你**曾经**走过路上学吗？Nǐ céngjīng zǒuguò lù shàngxué ma?

Did Mary **use to** come to your house for lunch?

玛丽**曾经**来过你家吃午饭吗？Mǎlì céngjīng láiguò nǐ jiā chī wǔfàn ma?

Did he **use to** be slim?

他**曾经**比较苗条吗？Tā céngjīng bǐjiào miáotiáo ma ?

Remember that 'used to' indicates a change from before until now, so (了) can be used:

I **used to** swim every day, but now I don't.

我**曾经每天**游过泳，但现在不游泳了。

Wǒ céngjīng měi tiān yóuguò yǒng, dàn xiànzài bù yóuyǒng le.

I **didn't use** to spend lots of money, but I do now.

我**曾经不会**花很多钱，但现在我花很多钱了。

Wǒ céngjīng bú huì huā hěn duō qián, dàn xiànzài wǒ huā hěn duō qián le.

Here are examples of statements regarding being 'used to doing' something:

I **am used to** living in this small city.

我**习惯**住在这座小城市。Wǒ xíguàn zhù zài zhè zuò xiǎo chéngshì.

He **is used to** walking 5 miles a day to school.

他**习惯**每天步行五英里去学校。Tā xíguàn měi tiān bùxíng wǔ yīnglǐ qù xuéxiào.

I **am not used** to giving my money away to strangers.

我**不习惯**把钱给陌生人。Wǒ bù xíguàn bǎ qián gěi mòshēngrén.

They **aren't used to** travelling to faraway places without their parents.

没有父母(陪伴)，他们**不习惯**到遥远的地方旅行。

Méi yǒu fùmǔ (péibàn) tāmen bù xíguàn dào yáoyuǎn de dìfāng lǚxíng.

When I was young, I **was used to** living in the countryside.

当我还小的时候，我**习惯**住在乡村。Dāng wǒ hái xiǎo de shíhòu, wǒ xíguàn zhù zài xiāngcūn.

I **never got used to** working in large groups.

我**从来没有习惯于**在大团体中工作。Wǒ cónglái měi yǒu xíguàn yú zài dà tuántǐ zhōng gōngzùo.

Are you used to living in this city?

你**习惯**住在这座城市吗？Nǐ xíguàn zhù zài zhè zuò chéngshì ma?

Yes, I **am used to** living in this city.

是的，我**习惯**住在这座城市。Shì de, wǒ xíguàn zhù zài zhè zuò chéngshì.

Were you **used to** working as a self-employed person?

你以前作为自由职业者习惯吗？Wǒ yǐqián zuòwèi zìyóu zhíyèzhě xíguàn ma?

No, I **wasn't used to** working as a self-employed person.

不，我**不习惯**当自由职业者。Bù, wǒ bù xíguàn dāng zìyóu zhíyèzhě.

Unit 1

(Subject + prepositional phrase + indirect object + direct object)

(Subject + time/when + prepositional phrase + verb)

Unit 2

举起来。我把我的书架举起来了。所有的狮子互相交战起来了。

如果我们一起工作起来，就有可能准时完成。

Unit 3

我认为这是很好的，你觉得呢？莫非他真的是一个可靠的人？

难道你是说你今晚不可能见我吗？

Unit 4

你知道这是什么吗？你知道这钱是谁的吗？

那边的人是谁？你知道那边的人是谁的吗？

Unit 5

I know 知道, 了解, 认识

I understand 理解, 得懂 I am clear 明白/知道了

Unit 6

我曾经跟我父母一起去过那里。我在冬天不曾旅行过。

With adjectives, 是, 有 and 在 do not use 过.

Unit 7

他习惯每天步行五英里去学校。

我不习惯把钱给陌生人。

It is important to know how to talk about something being 'like' something else.

This helps the listener imagine what something or someone is like:

This house **is like** a castle.

这座房子**就像**一座城堡。Zhè zuò fángzi jiù xiàng yī zuò chéngbǎo.

That view **is like** our countryside.

那里的风景**就像**我们的乡村。Nàlǐ de fēngjǐng jiù xiàng wǒmen de xiāngcūn.

It **is like** walking through a jungle.

这**就像**穿梭在丛林中。Zhè jiù xiàng chuānsuō zài cónglín zhōng.

He is so happy it **is like** he will never be sad again.

他很高兴，**就好像**他再也不会伤心一样。

Tā hěn gāoxìng, jiù hǎoxiàng tā zài yě bú huì shāngxīn yīyàng.

His car **looks like** my father's.

他的汽车**看起来像**我父亲的汽车。Tā de qìchē kànqǐlái xiàng wǒ fùqīn de qìchē.

She **sounds just like** an opera singer.

她**听起来像**一个歌剧歌手。Tā tīngqǐlái xiàng yī gè gējù gēshǒu.

This material **feels like** cotton.

这种材料**感觉像**棉花。Zhè zhǒng cáiliào gǎnjué xiàng miánhuā.

It **looks like** they are very cold.

他们**看起来**很冷。Tāmen kànqǐlái hěn lěng.

It **sounds like** madness to me.

这对我来说，**听起来**很疯狂。Zhè duì wǒ lái shuō, tīngqǐlái hěn fēngkuáng.

It **seems like** he isn't interested.

他**看起来**不感兴趣。Tā kànqǐlái bù gǎnxìng qù.

How to use 'There was...' in sentences:

There is a cup on the table.

桌子上面有一个杯子。Zhuōzi shàngmiàn yǒu yī gè bēizi.

There was a terrible smell in our fridge this morning.

今天早上冰箱里有一股难闻的气味。Jīntiān zǎoshàng bīngxiāng lǐ yǒu yī gǔ nánwén de qìwèi.

There isn't a student in the room.

在教室里没有一个学生。Zài jiàoshì lǐ méi yǒu yī gè xuéshēng.

There wasn't a window in our hotel room.

（以前）我们的酒店房间没有一扇窗户。(Yǐqián) wǒmen de jiǔdiàn fángjiān méi yǒu yī shàn
chuānghù.

There is some coffee in the cup.

杯子里面有一些咖啡。 Bēizi lǐmiàn yǒu yīxiē kāfēi.

There was still some milk in the jug on the table.

（以前）房桌子上的水壶里还有一些牛奶。

(Yǐqián) zhuōzi shàng de shuǐhú lǐ hái yǒu yīxiē niúnǎi.

There isn't any water in the glass.

杯子里面没有一点水。Bēizi lǐmiàn méi yǒu yī diǎn shuǐ.

There wasn't any water coming from the tap in the bathroom.

（以前）浴室里的水龙头里没有一点水。

(Yǐqián) yùshì lǐ de shuǐlóngtóu lǐ méi yǒu yī diǎn shuǐ.

Was there a bottle of Coca Cola in the fridge this morning?

今天早上冰箱里有一瓶可乐吗？Jīntiān zǎoshàng bīngxiāng lǐ yǒu yī píng Kělè ma?

Was there any fresh orange juice for breakfast this morning?

今天早餐有新鲜的橙汁吗？Jīntiān zǎocāi yǒu xīnxiān de chéngzhī ma?

How to use 'There were...' in sentences:

There are cats and dogs in the garden.

花园里有狗和猫。Huāyuán lǐ yǒu gōu hé māo.

There were some poor people living near our neighbourhood.

（以前）我们附近**住着一些**穷人。(Yǐqián) wǒmen fùjìn zhùzhe yīxiē qióngrén.

There aren't any children in the playground.

操场里没有一些孩子。Cāochǎng lǐ měi yǒu yīxiē háizi.

There weren't any police officers on the streets today.

今天这条街上**没有**任何警察。Jīntiān zhè tiáo jiē shàng měi yǒu rènhé jǐngchá.

There are some dogs in the park.

公园里有一些狗。Gōngyuán lǐ yǒu yīxiē gǒu.

There were some dirty clothes on my bedroom floor.

（以前）在我卧室地板上**有一些**脏衣服。(Yǐqián) zài wǒ wòshì dìbǎn shàng yǒu yīxiē zāng yīfú.

There aren't any books in the schoolbag.

书包里面没有任何本书。Shūbāo lǐmiàn měi yǒu rènhé běn shū.

There weren't any flowers on our balcony last month.

上个月我们的阳台**没有任何**鲜花。Shàng gè yuè wǒmen de yángtái měi yǒu rènhé xiǎnhuā.

Were there a lot of issues at work today, Honey?

亲爱的，今天工作中**有很多**问题吗？Qīnài de, jīntiān gōngzuò zhōng yǒu hěn duō wèntí ma?

Were there any troublesome children in your class this week?

这周你们班上**有**闹事的孩子吗？Zhè zhōu nǐmen bān shàng yǒu nàoshì de háizi ma?

How to use 'There will be...' and 'There won't be...' in sentences:

There will be an exciting TV programme on tonight.

今晚**将有**一个令人兴奋的电视节目。Jīnwǎn jiāng yǒu yī gè lìngrén xìngfèn de diànshì jiémù.

There will be many surprises at your birthday party.

你的生日聚会**将有**很多惊喜。Nǐ de shēngrì jùhuì jiāng yǒu hěn duō jīngxǐ.

There won't be a meeting before you start work here.

在你开始工作以前**不会**举行会议。 Zài nǐ kāishǐ gōngzuò yǐqián bú huì jǔxíng huìyì.

There won't be any problems with my homework this time.

这次我的作业**不会有任何**问题。Zhè cì wǒ de zuòyè bú huì yǒu rènhé wèntí.

Will there be a clown at the party?

聚会上**会有**一个小丑吗？Jùhuì shàng huì yǒu yī gè xiǎochǒu ma?

Yes, there will. No, there won't. 是的，有。 不，没有。Shì de, yǒu. Bù, měi yǒu.

Will there be any issues with your assignment, Paul?

保罗，你的任务**会有任何**问题吗？ Bǎoluó, nǐ de rènwù huì yǒu rènhé wèntí ma?

Yes, there will. No, there won't.

是的，有。 不，没有。Shì de, yǒu. Bù, měi yǒu.

Unlike present continuous tense in Mandarin, there is no use of (着) because there is no such tense in Mandarin:

I was jogging in the park this morning.

我今天早上在公园里慢跑了。Wǒ jīntiān zǎoshàng zài gōngyuán lǐ mànpǎo le.

I wasn't walking along the street last night.

我昨晚**没有**沿着街道散步。Wǒ zuówǎn méi yǒu yánzhe jiēdào sànbù.

They were preparing for their test all night.

他们整夜在为他们的考试做准备。Tāmen zhěng yè zài wèi tāmen de kǎoshì zuò zhǔnbèi.

They weren't playing computer games last night.

他们昨晚**没有**玩电脑游戏。Tāmen zuówǎn méi yǒu wán diànniǎo yóuxì.

Was he working last weekend?

他上个周末上班了吗？Tā shàng gè zhōumò shàngbān le ma?

Yes, he **was**. No, he **wasn't**.

是的，他是。不，他不是。Shì de, tā shì. Bù, tā bú shì.

Were you playing golf with friends yesterday?

你昨天和朋友一起打高尔夫了吗？Nǐ zuótiān hé péngyǒu yīqǐ dǎ gāoěrfū le ma?

Yes, I **was**. No, I **wasn't.**

是的，我是。不，我不是。Shì de, wǒ shì. Bù, wǒ bú shì.

It might be necessary to explain that you had planned to do something, but in the end you changed your mind and did not do what you had previously planned:

I **was going to** see her last night, **but** I was feeling so tired I didn't bother.

昨晚我**本来会**去见她，**但**我感到很累，所以我没有打扰。

Zuówǎn wǒ **běnlái huì** qù jiàn tā, **dàn** wǒ gǎndào hěn lèi, suǒyǐ wǒ méi yǒu dǎrǎo.

They **were going to** ask me to go with them, **but** they realised that I hated rock climbing.

他们**本来打算**让我和他们一起去，**但**他们意识到我讨厌攀岩。

Tāmen **běnlái dǎsuàn** ràng wǒ hé tāmen yīqǐ qù, **dàn** tāmen yìshìdào wǒ tǎoyàn pānyán.

We **were going to** travel to Singapore, **but** my sister became sick, so we cancelled.

我们**本来要**去新加坡旅行，**但**我妹妹病了，所以我们取消了。

Wǒmen **běnlái yào** qù Xīnjiāpō lǚxíng, **dàn** wǒ mèimei bìng le, suǒyǐ wǒmen qǔxiāo le.

My colleague **was going to** borrow my car, **but** his girlfriend lent him her car instead.

我的同事**本来打算**借我的车，**但**他的女朋友把车借给他了。

Wǒ de tóngshì **běnlái dǎsuàn** jiè wǒ de chē, **dàn** tā de nǚ péngyǒu bǎ chē jiè gěi tā le.

Fiona and Margaret **were planning to** go, **but** finally they decided not to go.

菲奥娜和玛格丽特都**本来计划**去，**但**终于他们一起确定了不去。

Fēiàonà hé Mǎgélìtè dōu **běnlái jìhuà** qù, **dàn** zhōngyú tāmen yīqǐ quèdìng le bú qù.

How to make questions asking, 'How long does it take...?' to get from one location to another:

How long does it take you to get to work?

你去上班**需要/有**多长时间？Nǐ qù shàngbān xūyào/yǒu duōcháng shíjiān?

It **takes** me about 10 minutes by car to get to work.

开车去工作**需要**大约10分钟。Kāichē qù gōngzuò xūyào dàyuē 10 fēnzhōng.

How long does it take to learn English?

学英语**需要/有**多长时间了？Xué Yīngyǔ xūyào/yǒu duōcháng shíjiān le?

It **takes** a few years to learn English.

学习英语**有**几年了。Xuéxí Yīngyǔ yǒu jǐ nián le.

How long does it take to get from your house to your school?

从你家到学校**需要**多长时间？Cóng nǐ jiā dào xuéxiào xūyào duōcháng shíjiān?

It **takes** me 20 minutes on foot from my house to my school.

从我家到学校步行**需要**20分钟。Cóng wǒ jiā dào xuéxiào bùxíng xūyào 20 fēnzhōng.

How long did it take you to drive to Shanghai?

你开车到上海**需要**多长时间？Nǐ kāichē dào Shànghǎi xūyào duōcháng shíjiān?

It **took** me roughly 5 hours to drive to Shanghai.

我开车到上海大约**需要**5个小时。Wǒ kāichē dào Shànghǎi dàyuē xūyào wǔ gè xiǎoshí.

How long will it take you to get to the airport tomorrow morning?

你明天早上到机场**需要**多少时间？Nǐ míngtiān zǎoshàng dào jīchǎng xūyào duōshǎo shíjiān?

I think it will **take** me about 30-35 minutes to get to the airport tomorrow morning.

我想我明天早上到机场大约**需要**30-35分钟。Wǒ xiǎng wǒ míngtiān zǎoshàng dào jīchǎng

                                   dàyuē xūyào sānshí zhì sānshíwǔ fēnzhōng.

Unit 8

这座房子就像一座城堡。

这种材料感觉像棉花。

Unit 9

今天早上冰箱里有一股难闻的气味。

（以前）浴室里的水龙头里没有一点儿水。

Unit 10

（以前）在我卧室地板上有一些脏衣服。

上个月我们的阳台没有任何鲜花。

Unit 11

今晚将会有一个令人兴奋的电视节目。

这次我的作业不会有任何问题。

Unit 12

我今天早上在公园里慢跑。

他们整夜在为他们的考试做准备。

Unit 13

昨晚我本来会去见她，但我感到很累，所以我没有打扰。

我的同事本来打算借我的车，但他的女朋友把车借给了他。

Unit 14

你去上班需要/有多长时间?

开车去工作需要大约10分钟。

There are quite a few ways to say 'almost' in Chinese, and here are the ways:

almost (差不多):

Our parents' jobs are **almost** the same.

我们父母的工作都**差不多**。Wǒmen fùmǔ de gōngzuò dōu chàbuduō.

These paintings are **almost/basically** the same price.

这些油画的价格几乎/基本上都**差不多**。Zhèxiē yóuhuà de jiàgé jīhū/jīběn shàng dōu chàbuduō.

almost (with 跟 and 和):

My best friend and I think **almost** the same way.

我**跟**我最好的朋友的想法**差不多**。Wǒ gēn wǒ zuìhǎo de péngyǒu de xiǎngfǎ chàbùduō.

This department store and that department store and **basically** the same.

这所百货商店**和**那所百货商店**差不多**。Zhè suǒ bǎihuò shāngdiàn hé nà suǒ bǎihuò shāngdiàn chàbuduō.

You can also add (差不多) to an adjective:

I am sure those clothes are **almost** the same size.

我肯定那些衣服**差不多大小**。Wǒ kěndìng nàxiē yīfú chàbuduō dàxiǎo.

Those boxes are **almost** the same weight.

那些盒子都**差不多重量**。Nàxiē hézi dōu chàbuduō zhòngliàng.

Another way to say 'almost' that means something almost happened but eventually it didn't:

I **almost** fell.

我**差点**摔倒。Wǒ chàdiǎn shuāi dào.

He **almost** lost his temper.

他**差点**发脾气。Tā chàdiǎn fā píqì.

Here are two other ways to say 'almost' in Chinese:

almost (差点儿):

I **almost** didn't buy it, but I did.

我**差点儿**没买，但我买了。Wǒ chàdiǎnr méi mǎi, dàn wǒ mǎi le.

I **almost** didn't understand, but I did.

我**差点儿**没听懂，但我听懂了。Wǒ chàdiǎnr méi tīngdǒng, dàn wǒ tīngdǒng le.

I was lucky because I **almost** bought it.

我很幸运，因为**差点儿**买它了。Wǒ hěn xìngyùn, yīnwèi chàdiǎnr mǎi tā le.

almost (几乎):

Almost every person has a computer.

几乎所有的人都有电脑。Jīhū suǒyǒu de rén dōu yǒu diànnǎo.

Almost all my colleagues prefer a shorter working week.

几乎每个同事都更喜欢更短工作周。Jīhū měi gè tóngshì dōu gèng xǐhuān duǎn gōngzuò zhōu.

I find it hard to sleep **almost** every night.

我发现**几乎**每个晚上都很难入睡。Wǒ fāxiàn jīhū měi gè wǎnshàng dōu hěn nán rùshuì.

To be able to do better than someone else (得过), and unable to do something (不过):

I am **able to** do better than him. 我比**得过**他。 Wǒ bǐ deguò tā.

I am **unable to** beat him. 我比**不过**他。 Wǒ bǐ búguò tā.

You can use verb + (得及) for 'able to', and (不及) for 'unable to':

I am **able to** come. 我来**得及**。 or　我会来。 Wǒ láidejí.　Wǒ huì lái.

I am **unable to** come. 我来**不及**。 or　我不会来。 Wǒ láibují.　Wò bú huì lái.

In order to say 'can even + verb' use (甚至都能):

I **can even** hear them screaming.

我**甚至都能**听到他们在大声尖叫。 Wǒ shènzhì dōu néng tīngdào tāmen zài dàshēng jiānjiào.

I **can even** taste the butter.

我**甚至都能**尝一下黄油。 Wǒ shènzhì dōu néng cháng yīxià huángyóu.

The use of the double (不) can be used to talk about the impossibility of something:

There's **no possibility** that I cannot go.

我不可能不去的。 Wǒ bù kěnéng bú qù de.

It is **not possible** that they don't understand.

他们不可能不理解的。 Tāmen bù kěnéng bù lǐjiě de.

There's **no way** you cannot write English.

你不可能不会写英文。 Nǐ bù kěnéng bú huì xiě Yīngwén.

Here are examples of how to talk about present and future possibility, and how to talk about being able or unable to do something in the past:

Present possibility (可能):

My mother **could** be at home now.

我妈妈现在**可能会**在家里。Wǒ māma xiànzài kěnéng huì zài jiā lǐ.

There **could** be some apples in the dining room.

在餐厅里**可能会**有一些苹果。Zài cāntīng lǐ kěnéng huì yǒu yīxiē píngguǒ.

Future possibility (未来可能):

Father **could** be in another city next week.

下周父亲**可能会**在另一座城市。Xià zhōu fùqīn kěnéng huì zài lìng yī zuò chéngshì.

There **could** soon be a few days off school.

学校**可能**很快就**会**放几天假。Xuéxiào kěnéng hěn kuài jiù huì fàng jǐ tiān jià.

Past simple tense (可以, 能, 不能):

I **could** walk to work yesterday without any problems.

昨天我**可以**步行去上班，没有问题。

Zuótiān wǒ kěyǐ bùxíng qù shàngbān, méi yǒu wèntí.

They **could** go shopping with their mother after they had finished their homework.

在那时间，他们完成家庭作业后**可以**跟他们的妈妈一起去购物。

Zài nà shíjiān, tāmen wánchéng jiātíng zuòyè hòu kěyǐ gēn tāmen de māma yīqǐ qù gòuwù.

She **couldn't** go out and play with some of her friends because she was too busy.

她**不能**跟她一些朋友一起出去玩，因为她太忙了。

Tā bù néng gēn tā yīxiē péngyǒu yīqǐ chūqù wán, yīnwèi tā tài máng le.

Present and past tense (得了, 不了):

able to finish 完成**得了** wánchéngdeliǎo

able to play it 踢**得了**足球 tīdeliǎo zúqiú

unable to finish 完成**不了** wánchéngbuliǎo

unable to change ideas 思想改**不了** sīxiǎng gǎibuliǎo

(得起) and (不起) are only used with specific verbs such as 'buy' or 'afford':

I **can/am able to afford** to buy this house. 我**买得起**这所房子。Wǒ mǎideqǐ zhè suǒ fángzi.

I **cannot/am unable to afford** to buy that villa. 我**买不起**那所别墅。Wǒ mǎibuqǐ nà suǒ biéshù.

For specific activities, 'was able to' (能够) and 'managed to' (设法) are used. It could be a single event in the past or events that were specific and not commonplace:

I **was able to** eat five bowls of rice for dinner tonight.

我今晚晚饭**能够**吃五碗米饭。

Wǒ jīnwǎn wǎnfàn **nénggòu** chī wǔ wǎn mǐfàn.

My father **was able to** purchase all the materials he needed to repair the garden fence.

我爸爸**能够**购买修理花园围栏的所有材料。

Wǒ bàba **néngòu** gòumǎi xiūlǐ huāyuán wéilán de suǒyǒu cáiliào.

They **were able to** carry their suitcases all around the airport.

他们**能够拿**他们的行李箱搬运到在机场各个地方。(各个地方 means 'everywhere')

Tāmen **nénggòu** ná tāmen de xínglǐxiāng bānyùndào zài jīchǎng gège dìfāng.

I **managed to** finish the marathon in a decent time.

我**设法**在一个合适的时间**完成**（**一场**）马拉松比赛。

Wǒ **shèfǎ** zài yī gè héshì de shíjiān **wánchéng** (yī chǎng) mǎlāsōng bǐsài.

They **just about managed to** lift their extremely heavy rucksacks.

他们**只是设法/挣扎**地抬起来了他们非常沉重的背包。

Tāmen zhǐshì shèfǎ/zhēngzhá de táiqǐlái le tāmen fēicháng chénzhòng de bèibāo.

He **didn't manage to** sell all his old stuff at the market.

他**未设法**在市场上卖所有的旧货。

Tā wèi shèfǎ zài shìchǎng shàng mài suǒyǒu de jiù huò.

Here are examples of using 'should/ought to' (应该) for the present and past:

In the present:

I **should** help my mother with the dinner.

我**应该**帮我妈妈做晚饭。Wǒ yīnggāi bāng wǒ māma zuò wǎnfàn.

I **shouldn't** shout out loudly in class.

我**不应该**在课堂上大喊大叫。Wǒ bù yīnggāi zài kètáng shàng dàhǎn dàjiào.

In the future:

I **should** stay at home next week so I can prepare for my big test.

下周我**应该**留在家里，以至于我可以好好准备重要的考试。

Xià zhōu wǒ yīnggāi liú zài jiālǐ, yǐ zhìyú wǒ kěyǐ hǎohǎo zhǔnbèi zhòngyào de kǎoshì.

I **shouldn't** be late for work any longer.

我**不应该**再工作迟到了。Wǒ bù yīnggāi zài gōngzuò chídào le.

In the present:

You **ought to** finish your work now.

你**应该**现在完成你的工作。Nǐ yīnggāi xiànzài wánchéng nǐ de gōngzuò.

She **ought to** bring it to me right now.

她**应该**马上把它拿来给我。Tā yīnggāi mǎshàng bǎ tā nálái gěi wǒ.

In the future:

They **ought to** come over to my house more often.

他们**应该**经常过来我的房子。Tāmen yīnggāi jīngcháng guòlái wǒ de fángzi.

I **ought to** go over and speak with my neighbours more often.

我**应该**经常过去和邻居说话。Wǒ yīnggāi jīngcháng guòqù hé línjū shuōhuà.

In Mandarin, the modal verb 'have to' (不得不) can be used as follows:

have to: (In the present):

Children **have to** go to school.

孩子们**不得不**去上学。Háizimen bùdé bú qù shàngxué.

People **have to** be polite in society.

在社会中人们**不得不**礼貌相待。Zài shèhuì zhōng rénmen bùdé bù lǐmào xiāngdài.

He has broken his arm. He **has to** go to hospital.

他摔断了手臂。他**不得不**去医院。Tā shuāi duàn le shǒubì. Tā bùdé bù qù yīyuàn.

have to: (In the past):

They **had to** run quickly to catch the bus.

他们**不得不**跑了很快去追公共汽车。Tāmen bùdé bù pǎo le hěn kuài qù zhuī gōnggòng qìchē.

I **had to** return the books to the library.

在那时，我**不得不**把书还给图书馆。Zài nà shí, wǒ bùdé bù bǎ shū huán gěi túshūguǎn.

My father **didn't have to** stay up late and wait for me to come home.

我父亲**没有必要**熬夜等我回家。Wǒ fùqīn méi yǒu bìyào áoyè děng wǒ huíjiā.

When you have no choice but to do something (所以别无选择只好):

I forgot to reserve a table, **so I have no choice but to** go to another restaurant.

我忘了预定一张桌子，**所以别无选择只好**找到了其他的饭店。

Wǒ wàng le yùdìng yī zhāng zhuōzi, suǒyǐ biéwú xuǎnzé, zhǐhǎo zhǎodào le qítā de fàndiàn.

My parents wouldn't give me any money, **so I had no choice but to** find a job.

在那时，我父母不会把钱给我，**所以别无选择只好**寻找了工作。

Zài nà shí, wǒ fùmǔ bú huì bǎ qián gěi wǒ, suǒyǐ biéwú xuǎnzé, zhǐhǎo xúnzhǎo le gōngzuò.

It is normal to use 'must' (必须) in everyday Mandarin. Saying that something 'must be' is simply only the speaker's opinion, and others might not necessarily agree:

must & mustn't:

You **must** come with me now.

你现在**必须**跟我来。Nǐ xiànzài bìxū gēn wǒ lái.

She **must** lose some weight because she is looking a little fat.

她**必须**减肥，因为她看起来有点胖了。Tā bìxū jiǎnféi, yīnwèi tā kànqǐlái yǒu diǎn pàng le.

They **mustn't** do that. They'll hit somebody.

他们**一定不能**那样做。他们会打人。Tāmen yīdìng bù néng nà yàng zuò. Tāmen huì dǎ rén.

You **mustn't** leave your clothes on the floor.

你**一定不能**把衣服留在地板上。Nǐ yīdìng bù néng bǎ yīfú liú zài dìbǎn shàng.

had to & didn't have to:

(At that time) Eric **had to** give me some money.

(在那时) 艾瑞克**不得不**给我一些钱。(Zài nà shí) Àiruìkè bùdé bù gěi wǒ yīxiē qián.

(At that time) they **had to** see what was under the car for themselves.

(在那时) 他们**不得不**自己去看车子底下有什么。(Zài nà shí) tāmen bùdé bù zìjǐ qù kàn chēzi dǐxia yǒu shénme.

She **didn't have to** spend so much money.

她**没必要**花那么多钱。Tā méi bìyào huā nàme duō qián.

I **didn't have to** write so much for my essay.

我**没必要**写太多散文。Wǒ méi bìyào xiě tài duō sǎnwén.

Unit 15

我们父母的工作都差不多。我差点摔倒。我差点儿没买，但我买了。

几乎所有的人都有电脑。

Unit 16

我比得过他。我比不过他。我来得及。or 我会来。我来不及。or 我不会来。

我甚至都能尝一下黄油。你不可能不会写英文。

Unit 17

我妈妈现在可能会在家里了。完成得了。

完成不了。 我买得起这所房子。我买不起那所别墅。

Unit 18

我今晚晚饭能够吃五碗米饭。

我设法在一个合适的时间完成（一场）马拉松比赛。

Unit 19

我应该帮我妈妈做晚饭。

你应该现在完成你的工作。

Unit 20

孩子们不得不去上学。

我忘了预定一张桌子，所以别无选择只好找到了其他的饭店。

Unit 21

你现在必须跟我来。他们一定不能那样做。他们会打人。

艾瑞克不得不给了我一些钱。我没必要写太多散文。

These are examples of how to say 'need to', 'might' and 'may' in different tenses.

need to (In the present):

You **need to** put those toys away. 你需要把这些玩具收起来。Nǐ xūyào bǎ zhèxiē wánjù shōuqǐlái.

You **don't need to** shout at me. 你没有必要朝着我大喊。Nǐ méi yǒu bìyào cháozhe wǒ dàhǎn.

might (In the present):

He **might** be sleeping right now. 他可能正在睡觉。Tā kěnéng zhèngzài shuìjiào.

She **might not** be in her office. 她可能不在她的办公室。Tā kěnéng bú zài tā de bàngōngshì.

might (In the future):

They **might** visit us next week.

他们可能下周来拜访我们。Tāmen kěnéng xià zhōu lái bàifǎng wǒmen.

Peter **might not** go to university when he is older.

当皮特老了，可能不会去上大学。Dāng Pítè lǎo le, kěnéng bú huì qù shàng dàxué.

may (In the present):

He **may** be shopping for a new suit now.

他可能正在购买一套新西装。Tā kěnéng zhèngzài gòumǎi yī tào xīn xīzhuāng.

She **may not** know why we are here.

她可能不知道为什么我们在这里。Tā kěnéng bù zhīdào wèi shénme wǒmen zài zhèlǐ.

may (In the future):

They **may** decide to stop practising together.

他们可能决定停止一起练习。Tāmen kěnéng juédìng tíngzhǐ yīqǐ liànxí.

She **may not** get married in the future.

她将来可能不会结婚。Tā jiānglái kěnéng bú huì jiéhūn.

The phrase 'you might as well...' (干脆/不妨) is used as follows:

There's nothing else to do, so I **might as well** go out tonight.

没有别的东西做，我**干脆/不妨**今晚出去玩。

Méi yǒu bié de dōngxī zuò, wǒ gāncuì/bùfáng jīnwǎn chūqù wán.

Are you bored? You **might as well** help me clean the car.

你很无聊吗？你**干脆/不妨**帮我清洁车。

Nǐ hěn wúliáo ma? Nǐ gāncuì/bùfáng bāng wǒ qīngjié chē.

If you have nothing to do next week, **you might as well** accompany us to the theatre.

如果下周你没有事情，就**干脆/不妨**陪我们去剧院。

Rúguǒ xià zhōu nǐ méi yǒu shìqíng, jiù gāncuì/bùfáng péi wǒmen qù jùyuàn.

If you get bored during your time off work, **you might as well** go on a short trip.

如果你在下班时间感到无聊，就**干脆/不妨**短途旅行。

Rúguǒ nǐ zài xiàbān shíjiān gǎndào wúliáo, jiù gāncuì/bùfáng duǎntú lǚxíng.

In the last two examples, (就) means 'then' and there is no need to repeat the pronoun.

It is necessary to know how to make suggestions and give orders:

Let's go outside to play.

让我们出去玩耍。Ràng wǒmen chūqù wánshuǎ.

Let's/Do not do that. It looks dangerous.

它看起来很危险，**不要**那样做。Tā kànqǐlái hěn wéixiǎn, bú yào nà yàng zuò.

Let's go to the beach. **让我们**一起去海滩吧。Ràng wǒmen yīqǐ qù hǎitān ba.

Please be quiet in class, Joe.

乔，**请**在课堂上保持安静。Qiáo, qǐng zài kètáng shàng bǎochí ānjìng.

Please turn to page 56 in your workbooks.

请你们把你们的练习本翻到第56页。Qǐng nǐmen bǎ nǐmen de liànxí běn fān dào dì 56 yè.

Please give me your last report.

请把你的上次报告交给我。Qǐng bǎ nǐ de shàng cì bàogào jiāo gěi wǒ.

Can you come over here, please? **你能**到这边来吗？Nǐ néngdào zhèbiān lái ma?

Could you give me a hand, please? **请你能**帮我一个忙吗？Qǐng nǐ néng bāng wǒ yī gè

máng ma?

Have a safe trip! 一路平安！Yílù píng'ān!

Have a great day! 祝你拥有美好的一天！Zhù nǐ yǒngyǒu měihǎo de yītiān!

Be careful! 小心！Xiǎoxīn!

Be on time! 要准时！Yào zhǔnshí!

Don't run along the corridor! 不要在走廊里奔跑！Bú yào zài zǒuláng lǐ bēnpǎo!

Don't eat in class! 不要在课堂上吃东西！Bú yào zài kètáng shàng chī dōngxī!

'not at all' (一点儿也不/一点都不/一点也不 + adj). The past tense uses (没) instead of (不):

Studying art isn't difficult **at all**.

学习美术**一点儿也不**难。Xuéxí měishù yīdiǎnr yě bù nán.

This Indian food isn't delicious **at all**.

这印度菜**一点儿也不**美味。Zhè Yìndù cài yīdiǎnr yě bù měiwèi.

I am sure that they don't know anything about her medical condition **at all**.

我相信他们对她的病情**一点儿也不**知道。Wǒ xiāngxìn tāmen duì tā de bìngqíng yīdiǎnr yě bù

zhīdào.

I don't believe him **at all**.

我**一点都**不相信他。Wǒ yī diǎn dōu bù xiāngxìn tā.

She can't speak Chinese **at all**.

她**一点都**不会说中文。Tā yī diǎn dōu bú huì shuō Zhōngwén.

I don't think he's clever **at all**.

我认为他**一点都**不聪明。Wǒ rènwéi tā yī diǎn dōu bù cōngmíng.

He didn't understand **at all**.

他**一点也**没理解。Tā yī diǎn yě méi lǐjiě.

I didn't exercise **at all**.

我**一点都**没锻炼。Wǒ yī diǎn dōu méi duànliàn.

When expressing 'after all', (毕竟) is used before pronoun:

Don't be angry, **after all** he's only 5 years old.

不要生气。他**毕竟**只五岁。Bú yào shēngqì. Tā bìjìng zhǐ wǔ suì.

After all it's summer, it will be hot every day.

毕竟是夏天，天天都很热。Bìjìng shì xiàtiān, tiāntiān dōu hěn rè.

There is another way to say 'Don't...!' (别). It is used when someone is not already doing it, but it is possible that the person or people might do it in the near or immediate future:

Don't move!

别动！ Bié dòng!

Don't leave the door open!

别开门！ Bié kāimén!

Don't speak loudly!

别说话得大声！Bié shuōhuà de dàshēng!

Don't interrupt me when I'm speaking!

我说着话的时候，**别**打扰我！

Wǒ shuōzhe huà de shíhòu, bié dǎrǎo wǒ!

If someone is already doing something that you do not like, you have to use the (别...了) construct:

Stop running around!

别四处跑了！Bié sìchù pǎo le!

Stop drinking that wine!

别喝那葡萄酒了！Bié hē nà pútáojiǔ le!

Don't shout at me!

别对我大喊大叫了！Bié duì wǒ dàhǎn dàjiào le!

John, **stop** asking me the same question!

约翰，**别**问我一样的问题了！

Yuēhàn, bié wèn wǒ yīyàng de wèntí le!

Don't blame... (不要怪):

Although he is late, **don't** blame him because his father drives slowly.

虽然他迟到了，可是这也**不要怪**他，因为他爸爸开车很慢。

Suīrán tā chídào le, kěshì zhè yě bú yào guài tā, yīnwèi tā bàba kāichē hěn màn.

Don't blame me!

不要怪我！Bú yào guài wǒ!

Don't blame this situation on me!

这个情况，**不要怪**我！Zhè gè qíngkuàng, bú yào guài wǒ!

There are many ways to express the adverb 'again' in Mandarin.

(再) is used when something is going to happen 'again' in the future:

Please come **again**. 请你**再**来/欢迎再来。Qǐng nǐ zài lái/huānyíng zài lái.

Can you say it **again**? 你可以**再**说一遍吗？Nǐ kěyǐ zài shuō yī biàn ma?

I will send it to you **again**！我会**再**发给你！Wǒ huì zài fā gěi nǐ!

When talking about something that happened in the past or is happening now, use (又...了):

I was late for school **again** today.

今天我**又**上学迟到**了**。Jīntiān wǒ yòu shàngxué chídào le.

Father is drunk **again**.

爸爸**又**醉**了**。Bàba yòu zuì le.

Did you forget to tell her **again**?

你**又**忘**了**告诉她吗？Nǐ yòu wàng le gàosù tā ma?

I **didn't** collect my report **again**.

我**又没**接收我的报告。Wǒ yòu méi jiēshòu wǒ de bàogào.

She didn't say anything to him **again**.

她**又没**跟他说什么话。Tā yòu méi gēn tā shuō shénme huà.

Luckily, our boss isn't here **again**.

幸运的是，我们的老板**又**不在这里。Xìngyùn de shì, wǒmen de lǎobǎn yòu bú zài zhèlǐ.

Are you not practising with him **again**?

你**又**不跟他在一起练习吗？Nǐ yòu bù gēn tā zài yīqǐ liànxí ma?

When you want to say that you think something is 'just about to happen', use (又 + verb 了):

My birthday is coming. I will receive lots of presents (**again**).

生日快到了，**又**能收到很多礼物了。Shēngrì kuài dào le, **yòu** néng shōudào hěn duō lǐwù le.

He's going to take us out for a meal (**again**).

他**又**要带我们出去吃饭了。Tā **yòu** yào dài wǒmen chūqù chīfàn le.

The measure word (遍) or (次) can be used to express 'once again':

Can you do it **again**? (once again)   Can I have one bottle **again**? (one more bottle)

你可以**再**做**一遍**吗？Nǐ kěyǐ **zài** zuò **yī biàn** ma?   你能**再**给我**一瓶**吗？Nǐ néng **zài** gěi wǒ **yī píng** ma?

Tell me **again**! (once again)   Can you send it to me **again**? (one more time)

再告诉我**一遍**！Zài gàosù wǒ yī biàn!   你能**再**寄给我**一次**吗？Nǐ néng **zài** jì gěi wǒ yī cì ma?

When expressing 'never again', (再也不...了) can be used:

I **never** want to read a romance novel **again**.

我**再也不**读浪漫小说了。Wǒ **zài yě bù** dú làngmàn xiǎoshuō le.

My father said I can **never** come home late **again**.

我爸爸说我**再也不**可以晚回家了。Wǒ bàba shuō wǒ **zài yě bù** kěyǐ wǎn huíjiā le.

When expressing 'again' or 'afresh', either (重新) or (再三) is used:

I think we need to start **again/afresh**.

我认为我们需要**重新**开始。Wǒ rènwéi wǒmen xūyào **chóngxīn** kāishǐ.

I will go back to college **again** next year.

我明年将**再次**回到大学。Wǒ míngnián jiāng **zài cì** huídào dàxué.

Unit 22

你需要把这些玩具收起来。你没有必要朝着我大喊。

他可能正在睡觉。他可能正在购买一套新西装。

Unit 23

没有别的东西做，

我干脆/不妨今晚出去玩耍。

Unit 24

让我们出去玩耍。乔，请在课堂上保持安静。请你们把你们的练习本翻到第56页。

你能到这边来吗？小心！不要在课堂上吃东西！

Unit 25

学习美术一点儿也不难。我一点都不相信他。他一点也没理解。

不要生气。他毕竟只五岁。

Unit 26

别动！别四处跑了！

不要怪我。

Unit 27

请你再来/欢迎再来。今天我又上学迟到了。我又没接收我的报告。

幸运的是，我们的老板又不在这里。她又没跟他说什么话。

Unit 28

他又要带我们出去吃饭了。你可以再做一遍吗？

我再也不读浪漫小说了。我认为我们需要重新开始。

There are many ways to express 'over and over again' as follows:

I thought about it **over and over again**.

我**想**了**又想**。Wǒ xiǎng le yòu xiǎng.

He read the book **over and over again**.

他这本书看了**一遍又一遍**。Tā zhè běn shū kàn le yī biàn yòu yī biàn.

Said told us **over and over again**, but we still didn't understand.

赛义德**一遍又一遍**地告诉我们，**但是**我们还是不明白。

Sàiyìdé yī biàn yòu yī biàn de gàosù wǒmen, dànshì wǒmen háishì bù míngbái.

We talked **over and over again**, but I still didn't believe him.

我们在一起**聊**了**又聊**，**但是**我还是不相信他。

Wǒmen zài yīqǐ liáo le yòu liáo, dànshì wǒ háishì bù xiāngxìn tā.

When using the past progressive tense, you can say that something happened again and again, then something else happens afterwards. (verb + 着 + verb + 着).

I was reading the newspaper **again and again**, then I got bored.

我**读着读着**报纸就感到厌倦。Wǒ dúzhe dúzhe bàozhǐ jiù gǎndào yànjuàn.

She jumped **again and again**, then she lifted some weights.

她**跳着跳着**，然后举起来一些重物。Tā tiàozhe tiàozhe, ránhòu jǔqǐlái yīxiē zhòngwù.

The repetition of classifiers can be expressed in different ways:

I asked him **again and again**.

我**一次又一次**问他。Wǒ yī cì yòu yī cì wèn tā.

I explained to him **again and again**.

我**一遍又一遍**地跟他解释。Wǒ yī biàn yòu yī biàn de gēn tā jiěshì.

Do it **little by little**.

一点一点做。Yī diǎn yī diǎn zuò.

Leave **one by one**.

一个一个离开。Yī gè yī gè líkāi.

There are some useful ways to say 'until' in Mandarin as follows:

I stayed on the beach **until** the sun went down.

我待/留在沙滩上，**直到**太阳下山。Wǒ dài/liú zài shātān shàng, zhídào tàiyáng xiàshān.

Basketball practice didn't finish **until** 9:00 p.m. last night.

昨晚篮球练习**直到**晚上九点**才**结束。Zuówǎn lánqiú liànxí zhídào wǎnshàng jiǔ diǎn cái jiéshù.

I was waiting for you **until** eleven p.m.

我**一直在**等你，**直到**晚上十一点。Wǒ yīzhí zài děng nǐ, zhídào wǎnshàng shíyī diǎn.

We have 30 minutes **until** the film **starts**.

到电影**开始**，我们还有三十分钟。Dào diànyǐng kāishǐ, wǒmen hái yǒu sānshí fēnzhōng.

I have one hour to prepare dinner **until** Father **arrives**.

到爸爸**回来**，我有一个小时准备晚饭。Dào bàba huílái, wǒ yǒu yī gè xiǎoshí zhǔnbèi wǎnfàn.

They had to wait **until** their teacher left.

到老师**离开**，他们不得不等了。Dào lǎoshī líkāi, tāmen bùdé bù děng le.

They will not order any more food **until** their relatives have arrived.

在亲戚**到达**以前，他们不会再点更多的菜。

Zài qīnqi dàodá yǐqián, tāmen bú huì zài diǎn gèngduō de cài.

She was relaxing in the sauna **until** late at night.

她在桑拿浴一直放松了**到**深夜。Tā zài sāngnáyù yīzhí fàngsōng le dào shēnyè.

The party was successful because it lasted **until** the next morning.

聚会很成功，因为它一直持续**到**第二天早上。

Jùhuì hěn chénggōng, yīnwèi tā yīzhí chíxù dào dì èr tiān zǎoshàng.

You can ask questions about 'why, where, who, when, what, whose, and how' something or somebody is now, was in the past, will be or is going to be in the future:

Do you know **where** she went?

你知道她去**哪里**了吗？ Nǐ zhīdào tā qù nǎlǐ le ma?

Do you know **where** she is going?

你知道她正要去**哪里**？ Nǐ zhīdào tā zhèng yào qù nǎlǐ?

She knows **where** he is going to be living.

她知道他要去**哪里**定居。 Tā zhīdào tā yào qù nǎlǐ dìngjū.

Do you know **what** I need?

你知道我需要**什么**吗？ Nǐ zhīdào wǒ xūyào shénme ma?

Does he understand **what** they are saying?

他明白他们在说**什么**吗？ Tā míngbái tāmen zài shuō shénme ma?

They realised **what** he did.

他们意识到他做**什么**。 Tāmen yìshídào tā zuò shénme.

Do you know **why** I am angry?

你知道我**为什么**生气了吗？

Nǐ zhīdào wǒ wèi shénme shēngqì le ma?

Does she know **why** they left so early?

她知道**为什么**他们那么早点离开了吗？

Tā zhīdào wèi shénme tāmen nàme zǎo diǎn líkāi le ma?

He understood **why** we were not there for long.

他理解**为什么**我们不能在那里很长时间。

Tā lǐjiě wèi shénme wǒmen bù néng zài nàlǐ hěn cháng shíjiān.

Do you know **who** that man is?

你知道那个男人是**谁**吗？Nǐ zhīdào nà gè nánrén shì shéi ma?

Did she tell you **who** came to her house last night?

她告诉你昨晚**谁**来她家了吗？Tā gàosù nǐ zuówǎn shéi lái tā jiā le ma?

The animal knew **who** its owner was.

动物知道它的主人是**谁**。Dòngwù zhīdào tā de zhǔrén shì shéi.

Do they know **when** the train leaves?

他们知道火车**何时**离开吗？Tāmen zhīdào huǒchē héshí líkāi ma?

Does he know **when** his parents are arriving?

他知道父母**何时**到达吗？Tā zhīdào fùmǔ héshí dàodá ma?

I am not sure **when** our father will arrive tonight.

我不确定我们爸爸今晚**何时**到达。Wǒ bú quèdìng wǒmen bàba jīnwǎn héshí dàodá.

Do you know **whose** jeans they are?

你知道这些牛仔裤是**谁的**？Nǐ zhīdào zhèxiē niúzǎikù shì shéi de?

I know **whose** coat that is.

我知道那件外套是**谁的**。Wǒ zhīdào nà jiàn wàitào shì shéi de.

I definitely don't know **whose** computer it is.

我肯定不知道那是**谁的**电脑。Wǒ kěndìng bù zhīdào nà shì shéi de diànnǎo.

Do you know **how** to get to Shanghai quickly?

你知道**如何**快速到达上海吗？Nǐ zhīdào rúhé kuàisù dàodá Shànghǎi ma?

My father didn't know **how** to repair my bicycle.

我父亲不知道**如何**修理我的自行车。Wǒ fùqīn bù zhīdào rúhé xiūlǐ wǒ de zìxíngchē.

He doesn't know **how** to achieve his ambitions.

他并不知道**何时**获得报复。Tā bìngbù zhīdào héshí huòdé bàofù.

These sentences are used when expressing two actions either at the same time or one after another.

Two events occurring one after another for past simple:

I **went** to the department store **to buy** some stylish jeans.

我**去了**百货商店**买**一些时尚的牛仔裤。

Wǒ qù le bǎihuò shāngdiàn mǎi yīxiē shíshàng de niúzǎikù.

They **studied** four languages to be able **to get** an interesting job.

他们**学会了**四种语言，（为了）能那份够**获得**有趣的工作。

Tāmen xuéhuì le sì zhǒng yǔyán, (wèile) néng nà fèn gòu huòdé yǒuqù de gōngzuò.

She **met** her friends at the gym **to do** some exercises.

她在体育馆**见到**她的朋友，**做**一些运动。

Tā zài tǐyùguǎn jiàndào tā de péngyǒu, zuò yīxiē yùndòng.

Two events occurring one after another for future simple:

I will **go** to Spain **to enjoy** the sunshine and beaches.

我会**去**西班牙，去**享受**阳光和沙滩。

Wǒ huì qù Xībānyá, qù xiǎngshòu yángguāng hé shātān.

They will definitely **come** to our villa **to appreciate** our home.

他们一定会**来**我们的别墅**欣赏**我们的家。

Tāmen yīdìng huì lái wǒmen de biéshù xīnshǎng wǒmen de jiā.

They are going **to take** a walk along the beach **to enjoy** the sea air.

他们要沿着海滩**散步**，**享受**海风。Tāmen yào yánzhe hǎitān sànbù, xiǎngshòu hǎifēng.

Lucy is going **to apply for** a visa **to travel** to the Philippines.

露西要**申请**签证**去**菲律宾**旅行**。Lùxī yào shēnqǐng qiānzhèng qù Fēilǜbīn lǚxíng.

Here are more examples of two events occurring one after another. The following examples use modal verbs. In some examples (以) is used. It has the same meaning as (来) when connecting one verb to another when the first activity is performed in order to achieve the next activity:

She **must try** harder in lessons **to get** a better score.

她**必须**在课程上努力学习，才能获得更好的成绩。

Tā bìxū zài kèchéng shàng nǔlì xuéxí, cáinéng huòdé gènghǎo de chéngjī.

I **want to buy** some new clothes **to wear** for my graduation party.

我**想**为毕业聚会**买**一些新衣服。Wǒ xiǎng wèi bìyè jùhuì mǎi yīxiē xīn yīfú.

He **would like to see** her **to thank** her for the flowers.

他**想见**她，**去感谢**她的鲜花。Tā xiǎngjiàn tā, qù gǎnxiè tā de xiānhuā.

I **might spend** some time with her **to tell** her some important things.

我**可能会花**一些时间跟她**分享**一些重要的事情。

Wǒ kěnéng huì huā yīxiē shíjiān gēn tā fēnxiǎng yīxiē zhòngyào de shìqíng.

Ben **could give up** smoking **to improve** his health.

本**应该戒**烟以**改善**他的健康状况。(以 means that one activity leads to another)

Běn yīnggāi jièyān yǐ gǎishàn tā de jiànkāng zhuàngkuàng.

I **should ride** a bicycle more often **to help** the environment.

我**应该**多**骑**自行车以**帮助**改善环境。

Wǒ yīnggāi duō qí zìxíngchē yǐ bāngzhù gǎishàn huánjìng.

Barbara **ought to go out** with her friends and **celebrate** her promotion.

芭芭拉**应该**跟朋友一起**出去庆祝**她的升职。

Bābālā yīnggāi gēn péngyǒu yīqǐ chūqù qìngzhù tā de shēngzhí.

There rules concerning the word 'just' in Mandarin are relatively difficult, so in order to use the word correctly and effectively, it is necessary to learn and understand each part of this unit.

There are 3 ways to say 'just' in Chinese: (刚), (刚刚) and (刚才). The first two (刚), (刚刚) are used interchangeably. They are both adverbs and placed before a verb and are used to place focus on the action given by the verb. The action is one that took place not long ago, perhaps 1 hour or 30 minutes prior to the person making the statement:

She **just** had dinner.

她**刚**吃晚饭。

Tā gāng chī wǎnfàn.

They **just** came back home.

他们**刚刚**回家。

Tāmen gānggang huíjiā.

I **just** managed to get a taxi.

我**刚**设法乘坐出租车。

Wǒ gāng shèfǎ chéngzuò chūzūchē.

Mother **just** finished work.

妈妈**刚刚**下班。

Māma gānggang xiàbān.

When talking about events that took place half a year ago or less, (刚) is used along with a duration statement at the end of the sentence:

I **just** saw him a few days ago.

我**刚**看到他几天以前。

Wǒ gāng kàndào tā jǐ tiān yǐqián.

Lucy **just** quit her job 1 month ago.

露西**刚**辞职工作一个月。

Lùxī gāng cízhí gōngzuò yī gè yuè.

We have **just** been engaged for half a year.

我们**刚**一起订婚半年。

Wǒmen gāng yīqǐ dìnghūn bàn nián.

He **just** set up a new business 4 months ago.

他**刚**建立一个新业务四个月。

Tā gāng jiànlì yī gè xīn yèwù sì gè yuè.

Some events take place 'just now' and (刚才...了) is used in such sentences. Unlike (刚/刚刚), it is a noun and can be used in the same way as (今天). Therefore, it focuses on the time between the event up to the present. It might be useful to note that when using (刚) and (刚刚) no (了) is required. This is because if an action took place one hour or 6 months ago, then the outcome of the action can be specified; if it occurred just now, the (了) indicates that an action has been completed, but it is too soon to know for sure if it did happen exactly as is stated by the speaker:

They were shouting at her **just now**.

他们**刚才**对她大喊了。

Tāmen gāngcái duì tā dàhǎn le.

I finished reading the book **just now**.

我**刚才**看完了这本书。

Wǒ gāngcái kànwán le zhè běn shū.

I am sure they bought some clothes **just now**.

我肯定他们**刚才**买衣服了。

Wǒ kěndìng tāmen gāngcái mǎi yīfú le.

Have you found it **just now**?

你**刚才**找到东西了吗?

Nǐ gāngcái zhǎodào dōngxī le ma?

The negative version of 'just now' is (刚才没), and the negative of 'just' is (不是刚/刚刚):

I **didn't** see her **just now**.

我**刚才没**看到她。

Wǒ gāngcái méi kàndào tā.

I **didn't** hear the teacher **just now**.

我**刚才没**听到老师说。

Wǒ gāngcái méi tīngdào lǎoshī shuō.

I **didn't just** arrive.

我**不是刚**到。

Wǒ bú shì gāng dào.

She **didn't just** learn how to play the guitar.

她**不是刚**学习弹吉他。

Tā bú shì gāng xuéxí tán jítā.

In complex sentences, (刚..., 就...了) can be used as follows:

I was **just** about to leave the house, (**when/then**) the phone rang.

我**刚**要离开家，**就**电话响了。

Wǒ gāng yào líkāi jiā, jiù diànhuà xiǎng le.

Frederick was just about to say that he loved her, (**when/then**) she dumped him.

弗雷德里克**刚**要说他爱她，她**就摆脱**他了。

Fúléidélǐkè gāng yào shuō tā ài tā, tā jiù bǎituō tā le.

We were just about to sit down for dinner, (**when/then**) our neighbour knocked on our door.

我们**刚**坐下来吃晚饭，我们的邻居**就**敲了我们的前门。

Wǒmen gāng zuòxiàlái chī wǎnfàn, wǒmen de línjū jiù qiāo le wǒmen de qiánmén.

(刚) can also be used to mean 'barely' or 'exactly' depending on the context:

These jeans **barely** fit me now.

这件牛仔裤，我穿小码的刚刚好。

Zhè jiàn niúzǎikù, wǒ chuān xiǎo

mǎ de gānggang hǎo.

The price is **exactly** 200,000 元.

价格**刚**二十万元。

Jiàgé gāng èrshí wàn yuán.

It might also be useful to say that something or someone is 'just like' something or someone else. In such an instance, (正像) before the pronoun or noun is used:

You look **just like** your father.

你看起来**正像**你爸爸。

Nǐ kànqǐlái zhèng xiàng nǐ bàba.

It is **just like** him to forget.

正像他忘记了一样。

Zhèng xiàng tā wàngjì le yīyàng.

Unit 29

我想了又想。

我读着读着报纸就感到厌倦。 我一次又一次问他。

Unit 30

我一直在等你，直到晚上十一点。

到电影开始，我们还有三十分钟。 她在桑拿浴一直放松了到深夜。

Unit 31

你知道她去哪里了吗？ 他们意识到他做什么。

你知道如何快速到达上海吗？

Unit 32

她在体育馆见到她的朋友，做一些运动。

我应该多骑自行车以帮助改善环境。

Unit 33

她刚吃晚饭。我刚设法乘坐出租车。

我刚看到他几天以前。

Unit 34

他们刚才对她大喊了。

我刚才没看到他。

Unit 35

我刚要离开家，就电话响了。这件牛仔裤，我穿小码的刚好。

价格刚二十万元。你看起来正像你爸爸。

It is useful to say that some event or situation is going to happen soon, and it is almost here.

(快...了) and (快到...了) are both used:

Christmas **is coming**. (Christmas is almost here.)

圣诞节**快到**了。 Shèngdànjié kuàidào le.

快要圣诞节了。 Kuàiyào Shèngdànjié le.

It's going to be hot **soon**.

很**快**会热**起来**。Hěn kuài huì rèqǐlái. (起来 indicates that an action is about to occur)

He's going to be drunk **soon**.

他**快**醉了。Tā kuài zuì le.

I am **about to** quit my job.

我**快**辞职了。Wǒ kuài cízhí le.

我**即将**辞职。Wǒ jíjiāng cízhí.

It's going to be my birthday **soon**. = It's almost my birthday.

我的生日**快到**了。Wǒ de shēngrì kuàidào le.

I am excited. Labour Day is **almost** here.

我很兴奋，劳动节**快到**了。Wǒ hěn xīngfèn, Láodòngjié kuàidào le.

Look at the sky. I think the rain is coming **soon**.

看天空，我想**快**要下雨了。Kàn tiānkōng, wǒ xiǎng kuài yào xiàyǔ le.

The verb 'to get' can often be used in English. Here are some examples of how it is used in Mandarin:

to **get** an email 收到邮件 shōudào yóujiàn

to **get** a job 找到工作 zhǎodào gōngzuò

to **get** somebody for somebody else (on the telephone) 联系上某人 liánxì shàng mǒurén

to **get** a haircut 理发 lǐfǎ   to **get** married 结婚 jiéhūn

to **get** divorced 离婚 líhūn   to **get** lost 迷路 mílù

to **get** pregnant 怀孕 huáiyùn

to **get/take** a taxi, bus 乘坐出租车，乘坐巴士 chéngzuò chūzūchē, chéngzuò bāshì.

to **get/take** a train, plane 乘坐火车，乘坐飞机 chéngzuò huǒchē, chéngzuò fēijī

to **get** to work 去上班 qù shàngbān

to **get** to some place 到达某个地方 dàodá mǒu gè dìfāng

to **get** home 回家 huíjiā

to **get on/off** a bus 上/下公共汽车 shàng/xià gōnggòng qìchē

to **get out/into** of a car 下车/上车 xià chē/shàng chē

Sometimes there is a change from one state to another. In these instances, you can say the following:

If I don't eat, I **will get** hungry.

如果我不吃，我**会感到**饥饿。

Rúguǒ wǒ bù chī, wǒ huì gǎndào jī è.

The weather **is getting** colder.

天气**越来越**冷了。

Tiānqì yuè lái yuè lěng le.

The days **are getting** shorter these days.

这些日子**越来越短**了。Zhèxiē rìzi yuè lái yuè duǎn le.

When we want to talk about something, but we do not know exactly who or what it is, we use 'indefinite pronouns':

There is **something** in this box.

这个盒子里有一些**东西**。Zhè gè hézi lǐ yǒu yīxiē dōngxī.

There was **something** special about that day.

那天有一些特别的**东西/意义**。Nà tiān yǒu yīxiē tèbié de dōngxī/yìyì.

Something is bothering me.

有一些**东西**困扰着我。Yǒu yīxiē dōngxī kùnrǎo zhe wǒ.

I need **somewhere** to live.

我需要找一个**地方**住。Wǒ xūyào zhǎo yī gè dìfāng zhù.

I must have lost my notebook **somewhere**.

我肯定把笔记本丢在**某个地方**了。Wǒ kěndìng bǎ bǐjìběn diū zài mǒu gè dìfāng le.

That city is **somewhere** in Australia.

这座城市是澳大利亚的**某个地方**。Zhè zuò chéngshì shì Àodàlìyǎ de mǒu gè dìfāng.

There is **someone** coming.

有人来了。Yǒu rén lái le.

There is **somebody** in that room.

在那间房间里**有一些人**。Zài nà jiān fángjiān lǐ yǒu yīxiē rén.

Someone stole my bicycle.

某人偷了我的自行车。Mǒurén tōu le wǒ de zìxíngchē.

I heard **someone** shouting.

我听到**某人**叫喊。Wǒ tīngdào mǒurén jiàohǎn.

Anything, anybody and anywhere (more examples of indefinite pronouns) are used for both questions and negative answers in the following way:

There isn't **anything** I can say about the film.

关于这部电影我**没有什么**可说的。Guānyú zhè bù diànyǐng wǒ méi yǒu shénme kě shuō de.

There isn't **anybody** in my family who can speak Chinese.

我家里**没有人**会说中文。Wǒ jiā lǐ méi yǒu rén huì shuō Zhōngwén.

There isn't **anywhere** in my city to buy a Lamborghini.

我的城市里**没有任何地方**可以买到兰博基尼。

Wǒ de chéngshì lǐ méi yǒu rènhé dìfāng kěyǐ mǎidào Lánbójīní.

Is there **anything** I can do to help?

有什么我可以帮忙的吗？Yǒu shénme wǒ kěyǐ bāngmáng de ma?

No, there isn't **anything** you can do to help.

不，你**没什么**可以帮上忙的。Bù, nǐ méi shénme kěyǐ bāng shàng máng de.

Is there **anybody** here who can help us?

这里**有人**可以帮助我们吗？Zhèlǐ yǒu rén kěyǐ bāngzhù wǒmen ma?

No, there isn't **anybody** here who can help.

不，这里**没有人**能提供帮助。Bù, zhèlǐ méi yǒu rén néng tígōng bāngzhù.

Is there **anywhere** for us to have some fun?

有什么地方可以让我们玩得开心/找乐子吗？

Yǒu shénme dìfāng kěyǐ ràng wǒmen wán de kāixīn/zhǎo lèzi ma?

No, there isn't **anywhere** for you to have any fun.

不，**没有任何地方**可以让你玩得开心。

Bù, méi yǒu rènhé dìfāng kěyǐ ràng nǐ wán de kāixīn.

There is **nothing** to do here.

这里**没什么**可做的。Zhèlǐ méi shénme kě zuò de.

There is **nobody** here to talk to about the problem.

这里**没有人**谈论这道问题。Zhèlǐ méi yǒu rén tánlùn zhè dào wèntí.

There is **nowhere** to go in this boring city.

这座无聊的城市**无处**可去。Zhè zuò wúliáo de chéngshì wúchù kě qù.

Is there **anything** to eat in the fridge?

冰箱里**有什么**吃的吗？Bīngxiāng lǐ yǒu shénme chī de ma?

No, there is **nothing** to eat in the fridge.

不，冰箱里**没有东西**可以吃。Bù, bīngxiāng lǐ méi yǒu dōngxī kěyǐ chī.

Is there **nothing** we can do?

我们什么都**做不了**吗？Wǒmen shénme dōu zuòbuliǎo ma?

Is there **anybody** in the garden right now?

现在花园里**有人**吗？Xiànzài huāyuán lǐ yǒu rén ma?

No, there is **nobody** in the garden right now.

不，现在花园里**没有人**。Bù, xiànzài huāyuán lǐ méi yǒu rén.

Is there **nobody** you can phone?

你**没有人**可以打电话吗？Nǐ méi yǒu rén kěyǐ dǎ diànhuà ma?

Is there **anywhere** for the children to play?

有**什么地方**是给孩子们玩耍的吗？Yǒu shénme dìfāng shì gěi háizimen wánshuǎ de ma?

No, there is **nowhere** for the children to play.

不，孩子们没有**什么地方**可以玩。Bù, háizimen méi yǒu shénme dìfāng kěyǐ wán.

Is there **nowhere** you can go?

你**无处**可去吗？Nǐ wúchù kě qù ma?

How to express 'whenever, whatever, whoever, however and wherever':

You can leave **whenever** you want.

你可以**随时**离开。Nǐ kěyǐ suíshí líkāi. or 你想走就走吧。Nǐ xiǎng zǒu jiù zǒu ba.

Come over **whenever** you want.

你想**什么时候**过来**就什么时候**过来。Nǐ xiǎng shénme shíhòu guòlái jiù shénme shíhòu guòlái.

You can drink **whatever** you want.

想喝什么**就**喝什么。Xiǎng hē shénme jiù hē shénme.

You can choose **whatever** you want.

想选什么就选什么。Xiǎng xuǎn shénme jiù xuǎn shénme.

It is your party. You can invite **whoever** you like.

这是你的聚会，你**想**请**谁就**请**谁**。Zhè shì nǐ de jùhuì, nǐ xiǎng qǐng shéi jiù qǐng shéi.

I am going to see **whoever** wants to go out tonight.

我要去看看有谁想今晚出去。Wǒ yào qù kànkan yǒu shéi xiǎng jīnwǎn chūqù.

I intend to travel **however** I like.

我**想怎么**打算旅行**就怎么**旅行。Wǒ xiǎng zěnme dǎsuàn lǚxíng jiù zěnme lǚxíng.

She is going to create art **however** she likes.

她**想**怎么创造艺术**就怎么**创造。Tā xiǎng zěnme chuàngzào yìshù jiù zěnme chuàngzào.

I will go **wherever** I want.

我**想**去**哪里就**去**哪里**。Wǒ xiǎng qù nǎlǐ jiù qù nǎlǐ.

They play snooker **wherever** they can.

他们**想在哪里**打斯诺克**就在哪里**打。Tāmen xiǎng zài nǎlǐ dǎ sīnuòkè jiù zài nǎlǐ dǎ.

There are two useful ways of adding adverbs to change the meaning of a verb (adv + 地 + verb) or (verb + 得 + adv). When using (verb + 得 + adv) the verb is replicated:

He runs **fast**.

他跑步**跑得很快**。

Tā pǎo bù pǎo de hěn kuài.

He **slowly** learned how to speak Chinese.

他**慢慢地**学习中文。

Tā mànman de xuéxí Zhōngwén.

He speaks **clearly**. 他说话说**得清楚**。Tā shuōhuà shuō de qīngchǔ.

He speaks English **quickly**. 他说英语说**得快**。Tā shuō Yīngyǔ shuō de kuài.

He rides a bicycle **slowly**. 他骑自行车骑**得慢**。Tā qí zìxíngchē qí de màn.

He did **well** in the Chinese test. 他语文考试都考**得很好**。Tā Yǔwén kǎoshì dōu kǎo de hěn hǎo.

He doesn't drive **quickly**. 他开车开**得不快**。Tā kāichē kāi de bú kuài.

She doesn't speak Chinese **fast**. 她说中文说**得不快**。Tā shuō Zhōngwén shuō de bú kuài.

Remember that 'fast' and 'hard' are both adverbs and adjectives:

He washes clothes **fast**. 他洗衣服洗**得很快**。Tā xǐ yīfú xǐ de hěn kuài.

This is a **fast** car. 这是一辆**快**车。Zhè shì yī liàng kuài chē.

He studies **hard** every day. 他每天**努力学习**。Tā měi tiān nǔlì xuéxí. (Fixed phrase, no 得 or 地)

This material is really **hard**. 这个材料**是真硬的**。Zhè gè cáiliào shì zhēn yìng de.

When using the adverb 'late', there is no need to use either of the above methods.

He sometimes comes home **late**. 他有时候**回家很晚**。Tā yǒu shíhòu huíjiā hěn wǎn.

I was **late** again for work this morning. 我今早又**工作迟到了**。Wǒ jīnzǎo yòu gōngzuò chídào le.

Unit 36

圣诞节快到了。or 快要圣诞节了。

我快辞职了。or 我即将辞职。

Unit 37

乘坐出租车，乘坐巴士汽车， 如果我不吃

我会感到饥饿。天气越来越冷了。

Unit 38

这个盒子里有一些东西。

有人来了。我需要找一个地方住。

Unit 39

有什么我可以帮忙的吗？我家里没有人会说中文。

我的城市里没有任何地方可以买到兰博基尼。

Unit 40

这里没什么可做的。 冰箱里没有东西可以吃。

这里没有人谈论这个问题。 不，孩子们没有什么地方可以玩。

Unit 41

你可以随时离开。想喝什么就喝什么。这是你的聚会，你想请谁就请谁。

我想怎么打算旅行就怎么旅行。我想去哪里就去哪里。

Unit 42

他跑步跑得很快。 他快地跑步。

他有时候回家很晚。我今早又工作迟到了。

Here are some examples of common types of adverbs used in everyday Mandarin:

She is **very happy**.

她**很**高兴。

Tā **hěn** gāoxìng.

They are **too busy**.

他们**太忙了**。

Tāmen **tài máng le**.

A **more expensive** watch.

一款**更贵**的手表。

Yī kuǎn **gèng guì** de shǒubiǎo.

The **most elegant** dress.

最优雅的连衣裙。

Zuì yōuyǎ de liányīqún.

This fish is **rather spicy**.

这条鱼**比较辣**。

Zhè tiáo yú **bǐjiào là**.

That is **quite an honest** opinion.

这是一个**相当诚实**的意见。

Zhè shì yī gè **xiāngdāng chéngshí** de yìjiàn.

He is an **especially happy** man. 他是**特别/尤其乐观**的男人。Tā shì **tèbié/yóuqí lèguān** de nánrén.

They are **especially fast** cars. 它们都是**特别快**的汽车。Tāmen dōu shì **tèbié kuài** de qìchē.

My bed is **especially comfortable**. 我的床**格外舒服**。Wǒ de chuáng **géwài shūfú**.

Those are **extremely pretty** clothes. 那些是**非常漂亮**的衣服。Nàxiē shì **fēicháng piàoliang** de yīfú.

It's **extremely crowded here**. 这里是**非常拥挤**的。Zhèlǐ shì **fēicháng yōngjǐ** de.

My mum's new house is **incredibly large**. 我妈妈的新房子**极其大**。Wǒ māma de xīn fángzi **jíqí dà**.

His football skills are **really amazing**. 他的足球技巧是**真好的**。 Tā de zúqiú jìqiǎo shì **zhēn hǎo** de.

There are myriad intensifiers in Mandarin: (adj + 死了) negative; (adj + 极了) positive; (多 + adj) positive; (这么/那么/真 + adj) both; (adj + 坏了) negative. Here are examples of their usage:

I am **so** tried. 我累**死了**。Wǒ lèi sǐ le.

I am **so** hungry. 我饿**死了**。Wǒ è sǐ le.

My mother is **so** worried. 我妈妈担心**死了**。Wǒ māma dānxīn sǐ le.

This weather is **so** perfect. 这个天气好**极了**。Zhè gè tiānqì hǎo jí le.

The countryside is **so** peaceful. 乡村宁静**极了**。Xiāngcūn níngjìng jí le.

The exam today was **so** difficult. 今天的考试难**极了**。Jīntiān de kǎoshì nán jí le.

She is **so** beautiful. 她**多**漂亮。Tā duō piàoliang.

I think they are both **very** clever. 我认为他们都**多**聪明。Wǒ rènwéi tāmen dōu duō cōngmíng.

He thinks his son is **so** special. 他想他儿子**多**特别。Tā xiǎng tā érzi duō tèbié.

He drives **so** quickly. 他开车**那么**快。Tā kāichē nàme kuài. (那么 subj is not present)

You speak **so** slowly. 你说话**这么**慢。Nǐ shuōhuà zhème màn. (这么 subj is present)

This suitcase is **so** heavy. 这把手提箱**这么**重。Zhè bǎ shǒutíxiāng zhème zhòng.

Your daughter is **so** intelligent. 你女孩子**真**聪明。Nǐ nǚ háizi zhēn cōngmíng.

Those cars are **so** luxurious. 那些辆车都**真**豪华。Nàxiē liàng chē dōu zhēn háohuá.

That villa is **so** spacious. 那所别墅**可真**宽敞。Nà suǒ biéshù kě zhēn kuānchǎng.

I am **terribly** tired. 我累**坏了**。Wǒ lèi huài le.

I am **terribly** hungry. 我饿**坏了**。Wǒ è huài le.

He is **terribly** angry. 他生气**坏了**。Tā shēngqì huài le.

It is polite to say something nice, but you might sometimes want to say something that could upset somebody. For example, you might want to tell a parent that his or child is not so clever.

To make an adjective sound less offensive, use (不怎么) + adj:

Unfortunately, your child **isn't so** clever.

不幸的是，你孩子**不怎么**聪明。Búxìng de shì, nǐ háizi bù zěnme cōngmíng.

Our mother **isn't very** talented at cooking.

我妈妈做饭**不怎么**好。Wǒ māma zuòfàn bù zěnme hǎo.

When somebody does not understand why you are or are not doing something, the intensifier (又不) or (又没) can be used:

You **definitely** don't like them. So why did you buy them?

你**又不**喜欢它们，买它们干吗？Nǐ yòu bù xǐhuān tāmen, mǎi tāmen gàn ma?

He **definitely** hasn't been before. How could he know if it is a nice place?

他**又没**去过，怎么知道好不好地方？

Tā yòu méi qùguò, zěnme zhīdào hǎo bù hǎo dìfāng?

If something has been achieved but only after a lot of effort (好容易...才) or (好不容易...才) can be used. The (才) means that something has been completed but only after great effort:

It **was with considerable difficulty** that I managed to purchase this diamond ring.

我**好不容易才**设法购买了这钻石戒指。

Wǒ hǎo bù róngyì cái shèfǎ gòumǎi le zhè zuànshí jièzhǐ.

Before coming to China, I **had a difficult time** applying for a visa.

回中国以前，我**好不容易才**申请签证。

Huí Zhōngguó yǐqián, wǒ hǎo bù róngyì cái shēnqǐng qiānzhèng.

A way to say 'extremely' (得很) for positive and negative adjectives:

My son is **extremely/incredibly** naughty.

我儿子调皮**得很**。Wǒ érzi tiáopí de hěn.

Their new house looks **extremely/incredibly** luxurious.

他们的新房子好像豪华**得很**。Tāmen de xīn fángzi hǎoxiàng háohuá de hěn.

Another way to say 'extremely' (adj + 坏了) for positive and negative expressions:

All the students felt **extremely** excited.

学生都感到兴奋**坏了**。Xuéshēng dōu gǎndào xīngfèn huài le.

Today's weather is **extremely** freezing.

今天天气冰冷**坏了**。Jīntiān tiānqì bīnglěng huài le.

For negative expressions (adj + 得不得了) can be used:

My boss is **awfully/terribly** loud.

我的老板大声**得不得了**。Wǒ de lǎobǎn dàshēng dé bùdeliǎo.

He is **awfully/terribly** impolite.

他无礼**得不得了**。Tā wúlǐ dé bùdeliǎo.

You might want to say that somebody or something is 'not bad' or 'okay', so either (还可以) or (还不错) can be used:

Your Chinese is okay. 你的中文**还不错**。 Nǐ de Zhōngwén hái búcuò.

Her English is okay. 她的英文**还可以**。Tā de Yīngwén hái kěyǐ.

You can emphasise an adjective by replicating it:

Today is hot.

今天**热热的**。Jīntiān rèrè de.

He looks fat these days.

到目前为止，他看起来**胖胖的**。Dào mùqián wéizhǐ, tā kànqǐlái pàngpang de.

too (太…了):

This house is **too** large.

这所房子**太**大**了**。Zhè suǒ fángzi tài dà le.

These people are **too** unhealthy.

这些人**太**不健康**了**。Zhèxiē rén tài bú jiànkāng le.

really that + adj (有那么):

Does this ring **really** cost **that** much?

这枚戒指**有那么**贵吗？Zhè méi jièzhǐ yǒu nàme guì ma?

Is this wine **really that** good?

这葡萄酒**有那么**好吗？Zhè pútáojiǔ yǒu nàme hǎo ma?

Adverbs are essential to add depth of meaning, so here are examples of useful adverbs.

originally (原来) or (本来):

I **originally** came from England, then I moved to the US.

我**原来**来自英国，然后我搬家到美国。

Wǒ yuánlái láizì Yīngguó, ránhòu wǒ bānjiā dào Měiguó.

We were **originally** enemies, but we gradually became good friends.

我们**原来**是敌人，但是渐渐地成为了好朋友。

Wǒmen yuánlái shì dírén, dànshì jiànjian de chéngwéi le hǎo péngyǒu.

I **originally** planned to stay in Beijing, but finally I decided to come back to Shanghai.

我**本来打算**呆在北京，可是最终我决定了回到上海。

Wǒ běnlái dǎsuàn dāi zài Běijīng, kěshì zuìzhōng wǒ juédìng le huídào Shànghǎi.

So it was my daughter.

原来是我女儿。Yuánlái shì wǒ nǚ'ér.

So it turns out that you're stupid.

原来你很笨。Yuánlái nǐ hěn bèn.

suddenly/all of a sudden (一下子) or (突然) can be used:

All of a sudden, the baby stopped crying.

婴儿**一下子/突然**停止了哭泣。Yīng'ér yīxià zi/tūrán tíngzhǐ le kūqì.

Suddenly he became very angry.

他**一下子/突然**变得很生气。Tā yīxià zi/tūrán biàn de hěn shēngqì.

Finally I understood all of it.

最后我一下子**就**明白了。Zuìhòu wǒ yīxià zi jiù míngbái le.

I **finally** know.

我**终于**知道了。Wǒ zhōngyú zhīdào le.

They **finally** arrived in Shanghai.

他们**终于**到上海了。Tāmen zhōngyú dào Shànghǎi le.

I had **repeatedly** told him not to slam the door.

我**再三**告诉他不要关门关。Wǒ zàisān gàosù tā bú yào guānmén guān.

They have all **repeatedly** been warned by the police not to go to that derelict building.

他们被警察**一再**警告不可以去那栋废弃的大楼。

Tāmen bèi jǐngchá yīzài jǐnggào bù kěyǐ qù nà dòng fèiqì de dàlóu.

I will **immediately** pick up those important documents.

我马上会拾起那些重要的文件。Wǒ mǎshàng huì shíqǐ nàxiē zhòngyào de wénjiàn.

So, did he return **immediately** after finishing his presentation?

陈述完成以后，他**立刻**回来了吗？Chénshù wánchéng yǐhòu, tā lìkè huílái le ma?

Because I have little spare time, I try to travel **conveniently**.

因为我有很少空闲时间，就尝试**顺便**旅行。

Yīnwèi wǒ yǒu hěn shǎo kòngxián shíjiān, jiù chángshì shùnbiàn lǚxíng.

He **conveniently** never mentioned he wasn't at work all week last week.

他**若无其事地**从没提上个星期他全周没在工作。

Tā ruòwú qíshì de cóngméi tí shàng gè xīngqī tā quánzhōu méi zài gōngzuò.

When using either 'before' or 'after' to explain a sequence of events, there are some absolute rules that must be adhered to in order to use them correctly.

Consider a sequence of events for a habitual activity using 'before' (以前):

Before I go to high school, I want to go to Europe and travel.

我上高中**以前**，我想去欧洲旅行。Wǒ shàng gāozhōng yǐqián, wǒ xiǎng qù Ōuzhōu lǚxíng.

Before she eats breakfast, she usually washes her face.

她吃早餐**以前**，她经常洗脸。Tā chī zǎocān yǐqián, tā jīngcháng xǐliǎn.

Consider a sequence of events for a habitual activity using 'after (以后):

After I finish class, I go to the library.

我下(了)课**以后**，就去图书馆。Wǒ xià (le) kè yǐhòu, jiù qù túshūguǎn.

After they eat lunch, they often play basketball.

他们吃(了)中饭**以后**，就通常一起打篮球。

Tāmen chī (le) zhōngfàn yǐhòu, jiù tōngcháng yīqǐ dǎ lánqiú.

When using 'before' in the present, there is no need to use (了), but when using 'after' in the present, (了) is required since one event finishes before another starts. Therefore, the (了) indicates a completed action.

Now consider using 'after' and 'before' in conjunction with a future simple statement:

Before we go, we **will** prepare our things.

我们去**以前**，(我们) **会**准备东西。Wǒmen qù yǐqián, (wǒmen) huì zhǔnbèi dōngxī.

Before you can purchase your new car, you **will** need to save for a long time.

你购买新汽车**以前**，(你) **会**必要省很多时间钱。

Nǐ gòumǎi xīn qìchē yǐqián, (nǐ) huì bìyào shěng hěn duō shíjiān qián.

After we eat, we **will** go to the shopping centre.

我们吃(了)饭**以后**，**就**去购买中心。Wǒmen chī (le) fàn yǐhòu, jiù qù gòumǎi zhōngxīn.

After you apologise, you can relax.

你道(了)歉**以后**，**就**可以放松一下。Nǐ dào (le) qiàn yǐhòu, jiù kěyǐ fàngsōng yī xià.

When using 'before', there is no (了) and 'will' is written as (会); when using 'after', (了) has to be used as before to show that when one event finishes another starts, and 'will' is written as (就). In addition, (才) can be used in conjunction with (以后) to state that something happens 'only after' something has been completed:

After you have finished your assessment, (only) **then** you can leave the classroom.

你完成了股价**以后**，才可以离开教室。 Nǐ wánchéng le gǔjià yǐhòu, cái kěyǐ líkāi jiàoshì.

After they have a meeting, (only) **then** can they finish work.

他们开了会**以后**，才可以下班。Tāmen kāi le huì yǐhòu, cái kěyǐ xiàbān.

When using both 'after' and 'before' in the past, there are additional rules for the usage of (了).

Please note that (住) has to go before the (在) in a simple clause:

Before I came to China, I **lived** in London.

我来中国**以前**，我**住**在伦敦。Wǒ lái Zhōngguó yǐqián, wǒ zhù zài Lúndūn.

I **studied** really hard **before** the test.

我在考试**以前**，真的努力**学习了**。Wǒ zài kǎoshì yǐqián, zhēn de nǔlì xuéxí le.

You cannot put (了) in the clause containing (以前); however, you have to put (了) in the clause containing (以后):

After the movie had finished, I left the cinema.

电影结束**了以后**，**就**离开了电影院。Diànyǐng jiéshù le yǐhòu, jiù líkāi le diànyǐngyuàn.

After she bought ice cream, she watched television.

她买了冰淇淋**以后**，**就**看电视了。 Tā mǎi le bīngqílín yǐhòu, jiù kàn diànshì le.

(The 了 can go after an object if the verb only has one character)

After we all arrived home, we drank a few bottles of beer.

我们都到家**了以后**，**就**喝了几瓶啤酒。Wǒmen dōu dào jiā le yǐhòu, jiù hē le jǐ píng píjiǔ.

After I finished university, I wanted to travel the world.

我毕业**了**大学**以后**，**就**想周游世界。Wǒ bìyè le dàxué yǐhòu, jiù xiǎng zhōuyóu shìjiè.

(There is no 了 in the second clause because it was a desire, not an actual completed action)

There is another instance when using (了) two times is necessary, but for a different reason:

After I ate some Chinese medicine, I felt better.

我吃了中药以后，就好了。

Wǒ chī le Zhōngyào yǐhòu, jiù hǎo le.

After I decided to close the window, the room became warmer.

我确定关了窗户以后，房间**就**变暖了。

Wǒ quèdìng guān le chuānghù yǐhòu, fángjiān jiù biàn nuǎn le.

In these sentences, the (了) in the second clause indicates a change in state, not a completion of another action. See unit 136.

afterwards/later (后来) only used for past tense:

She quit her job, and **afterwards** she found a better one.

她辞职了，**后来**找到了更好的工作。

Tā cízhí le, hòulái zhǎodào le gènghǎo de gōngzuò.

(The 了 appears in both clauses because they both act as independent clauses)

He used to be an athlete. **Afterwards** he opened a company.

他曾经是一名运动员，**后来**开了一家公司。

Tā céngjīng shì yī míng yùndòng yuán, hòulái kāi le yī jiā gōngsī.

(There is no 了 in the first clause, because when using 曾经, there is no 了 or 过)

When it is 'easy to do something', use (好 + verb + 的):

It's easy to cook.

做饭**好做的**。Zuòfàn hǎo zuò de.

It's easy to read Chinese.

中文**好读的**。Zhōngwén hǎo dú de.

It's easy to ride a horse.

骑马**好骑的**。Qí mǎ hǎo qí de.

hard to do something (难做); no way I can do it (没有办法):

It's hard to understand the new teacher. There's no way to understand him.

很难理解新老师。**没有办法听**得懂他。

Hěn nán lǐjiě xīn lǎoshī. Méi yǒu bànfǎ tīngdedǒng tā.

It's hard to write so many Chinese characters.

写那么多汉字**很难**。**没有办法写**那么多汉字。

Xiě nàme duō hànzì hěn nán. Méi yǒu bànfǎ xiě nàme duō hànzì.

as much as possible (尽力以):

I must do **as much as possible** to make sure I win the match.

我必须**尽力以**确保我赢得比赛。Wǒ bìxū jìnlì yǐ quèbǎo wǒ yíngdé bǐsài.

My father always did **as much as he could** to help me with my studies.

我爸爸一直**尽力以**帮助我的学习。Wǒ bàba yīzhí jìnlì yǐ bāngzhù wǒ de xuéxí.

How to use 'enough' (足够) in sentences. The (来) means 'in order to' in the following:

There is **enough time** to finish the job.

有**足够的时间**来完成这项工作。Yǒu zúgòu de shíjiān lái wánchéng zhè xiàng gōngzuò.

There are **enough people** to make a football team.

有**足够的人**来组建一支足球队。Yǒu zúgòu de rén lái zǔjiàn yī zhī zúqiú duì.

There **isn't enough** sugar in the bowl.

碗里**没有足够**的糖。Wǎn lǐ méi yǒu zúgòu de táng.

There **aren't enough** chairs for all our guests.

没有足够的椅子给我们所有的客人。Méi yǒu zúgòu de yǐzi gěi wǒmen suǒyǒu de kèrén.

There **weren't enough** shops in the city to buy anything.

城市里**没有足够**的商店去买所有东西。

Chéngshì lǐ méi yǒu zúgòu de shāngdiàn qù mǎi suǒyǒu dōngxī.

Was **there enough** juice in the fridge?

冰箱里有**足够多**的果汁吗？Bīngxiāng lǐ yǒu zúgòu duō de guǒzhī ma?

I am **strong enough** to carry that bag.

我**足够强壮**以至于可以搬运那个包。Wǒ zúgòu qiángzhuàng yǐ zhìyú kěyǐ bānyùn nà gè bāo.

The students are **clever enough** to go to university.

学生都**足够聪明**以至于可以去最好的大学。Xuéshēng dōu zúgòu cōngmíng yǐ zhìyú kěyǐ qù

dàxué.

I have **enough experience** for this type of job.

我有**足够的经验**来完成这类工作。Wǒ yǒu zúgòu de jīngyàn lái wánchéng zhè lèi gōngzuò.

I think that shirt is **big enough** for you to wear.

我觉得衬衫**足够大**，你穿得下。Wǒ juéde chènshān zúgòu dà, nǐ chuān dé xià.

Making comparisons between things is an essential aspect of any language. Here are examples of changing adjectives into comparative adjectives.

To show a comparison (比) is used:

My father is **tall**.

我爸爸是高的。Wǒ bàba shì gāo de. 我爸爸高。Wǒ bàba gāo.

My father is **taller than** me.

我爸爸**比**我**高**。Wǒ bàba bǐ wǒ gāo.

This computer game is **fast**.

这个电脑游戏是快的。Zhè gè diànnǎo yóuxì shì kuài de.

This computer game is **faster than** that one.

这个电脑游戏**比**那个**快**。Zhè gè diànnǎo yóuxì bǐ nà gè kuài.

If the adjective has two or more syllables, there is no change in the use of (比):

This apple is **delicious**. 这个苹果（很）美味。Zhè gè píngguǒ (hěn) měiwèi.

Those apples are **more delicious than** these ones.

那些苹果**比**这些苹果**更美味**。Nàxiē píngguǒ bǐ zhèxiē píngguǒ gèng měiwèi.

That dress is **expensive**. 那件连衣裙（很）贵。Nà jiàn liányīqún (hěn) guì.

That dress is **more expensive than** the other one.

那件连衣裙**比**另一件**更贵**。Nà jiàn liányīqún bǐ lìng yī jiàn gèng guì.

I think swans are **elegant**.

我认为天鹅很优雅。Wǒ rènwéi tiān'é hěn yōuyǎ.

I think swans are **more elegant than** ducks.

我认为天鹅**比**鸭子**更优雅**。Wǒ rènwéi tiān'é bǐ yāzǐ gèng yōuyǎ.

Unit 43

他很高兴。他们太忙了。

他是特别/尤其乐观的男人。他的足球技巧真好的。

Unit 44

adj + 死了；adj + 极了；adj + 坏了；adj + 得很；adj + 得不得了还 + adj；有那么 + adj；

又不 + adj；真 + adj；这么/那么 + adj；多 + adj 好不容易 + verb；热热的；胖胖的

Unit 45

本来/原来；so 原来 一下子/突然；一下子就；

再三/一再；马上/立刻；顺便/若无其事地

Unit 46

after: 我...以前，...；我...以前，...会...；我...以前，...了

before: 我...以后，...就...；我...以后，...才...；我...了以后，...就...了。我...了来后，...了

Unit 47

做饭好做的。写那么多汉字很难。没办法写那么多汉字。

我爸爸一直尽力以帮助我的学习。

Unit 48

有足够的时间来完成这项工作。碗里没有足够的糖。

我有足够的经验来完成这类工作。

Unit 49

我爸爸比我高。

那件连衣裙比另一件更贵。

When using comparative adjectives, you might wish to add further meaning by adding 'much' (得多) or 'a little more' (一点) to the comparative adjectives:

The weather today is **much hotter than** yesterday.

今天的天气**比**昨天**热得多**。Jīntiān de tiānqì bǐ zuótiān rè de duō.

This sports car is **much quicker than** that one.

这辆跑车**比**那辆**快得多**。Zhè liàng pǎochē bǐ nà liàng kuài de duō.

Physics is **much more difficult than** biology.

物理学**比**生物学**难得多**。Wùlǐ xué bǐ shēngwù xué nán de duō.

My sister is **much more hardworking than** I am.

我姐妹**比**我**用功得多**。Wǒ jiěmèi bǐ wǒ yònggōng de duō.

I think that house is **a little larger than** our one.

我认为那所房子**比**我们的**大一点**。Wǒ rènwéi nà suǒ fángzi bǐ wǒmen de dà yī diǎn.

That table is definitely **a little smaller than** this one.

那张桌子肯定**比**这张桌子**小一点**。Nà zhāng zhuōzi kěndìng bǐ zhè zhāng zhuōzi xiǎo yī diǎn.

She is **a little more patient than** I am.

她**比**我**耐心一点**。Tā bǐ wǒ nàixīn yī diǎn.

I am **a little less educated than** my wife.

我的**教育**程度**不如**我太太。Wǒ de jiàoyù chéngdù bùrú wǒ tàitai.

我的**教育**程度**比**我太太**低**。Wǒ de jiàoyù chéngdù bǐ wǒ tàitai dī.

You might want to say that something or someone is 'even more (更) + adj' than:

Japanese guitars are expensive, but American guitars are **even more expensive**.

日本吉他很贵，（但是）美国吉他**更贵**。

Rìběn jítā hěn guì, (dànshì) Měiguó jítā **gèng guì**.

My new suit is luxurious, but yours is **even more luxurious**.

我的西装豪华，（但是）你的**更豪华**。

Wǒ de xīzhuāng háohuá, (dànshì) nǐ de **gèng háohuá**.

I am sure that my father **prefers** outdoor activities **even more than** my brother.

我确定我爸爸**比**我哥哥**更喜欢**户外活动。

Wǒ quèdìng wǒ bàba **bǐ** wǒ gēge **gèng xǐhuān** hùwài huódòng.

They really enjoy singing songs at Christmas, but my parents **enjoy** it **even more than** me.

他们真的很享受在圣诞节唱歌，（但是）我父母**比**我**更享受**。

Tāmen zhēn de hěn xiǎngshòu zài Shèngdànjié chànggē, (dànshì) wǒ fùmǔ bǐ wǒ

gèng xiǎngshòu.

When using verbs, adding further information to those verbs to improve the expressiveness of the sentence is an effective way to create sentences:

My father **drives more than** my mother.

我爸爸比我妈妈开**车开得多**。Wǒ bàba bǐ wǒ māma kāichē kāi de duō.

She **runs less than** me.

她比我跑**步跑得少**。Tā bǐ wǒ pǎobù pǎo de shǎo.

她跑步**跑得比**我少。Tā pǎobù pǎo de bǐ wǒ shǎo.

I **eat more food than** you.

我比你**吃得多**。Wǒ bǐ nǐ chī de duō.

我吃饭**吃得比**你多。Wǒ chīfàn chī de bǐ nǐ duō.

I can **swim more quickly than** my best friend.

我比我最好朋友游**泳游得快**。Wǒ bǐ wǒ zuìhǎo péngyǒu yóuyǒng yóu de kuài.

A tortoise **eats more slowly than** a cheetah.

乌龟比猎豹吃饭**吃得慢**。Wūguī bǐ lièbào chīfàn chī de màn.

Louise can **work more effectively than** Jane.

路易斯可以**比**简更有**效率地工作**。Lùyìsī kěyǐ bǐ Jiǎn gèng yǒu xiàolǜ de gōngzuò.

I can **drive this car much more quickly than** you can.

我能比你**更快地驾驶**这辆汽车。Wǒ néng bǐ nǐ gèng kuài de jiàshǐ zhè liàng qìchē.

He always **dresses much more appropriately than** I do.

他总是**比**我**穿得更合适**。Tā zǒngshì bǐ wǒ chuān de gèng héshì.

They managed to **do the work much more efficiently than** me.

他们**比**我**更有效地完成了**工作。Tāmen bǐ wǒ gèng yǒuxiào de wánchéng le gōngzuò.

The following are ways to say 'noun + even/even more + adverb + than + noun', 'verb + even more + than' and 'verb + even more + adverb + than + noun':

This painting is **even better than** that one.

这幅油画**比**那幅油画**更好**。Zhè fú yóuhuà bǐ nà fú yóuhuà gèng hǎo.

That room is **even colder than** this one.

那间房间**比**这间房间**更冷**。Nà jiān fángjiān bǐ zhè jiān fángjiān gèng lěng.

Those pieces of furniture are **even more expensive than** these.

那些家具**比**这些家具**更贵**。Nàxiē jiājù bǐ zhèxiē jiājù gèng guì.

She is **even more beautiful than** her picture.

她长得**比**照片上**更漂亮**。Tā zhǎng de bǐ zhàopiàn shàng gèng piàoliang.

He **likes** chocolate **even more than** she does.

他**比**她**更喜欢**巧克力。Tā bǐ tā gèng xǐhuān qiǎokèlì.

They **can play** badminton **even better than** I can.

他们打羽毛球打得**比**我**更好**。Tāmen dǎ yǔmáoqiú dǎ de bǐ wǒ gèng hǎo.

They can **generate** business **even more quickly** than I can.

他们**比**我**更快**地开展业务。Tāmen bǐ wǒ gèng kuài de kāizhǎn yèwù.

Edward can **reduce** his prices **even more generously** than we can.

爱德华**比**我们**更慷慨**地降低价格。Àidéhuá bǐ wǒmen gèng kāngkǎi de jiàngdī jiàgé.

You might want to say that two things are equal or the same:

My father is **the same age as** your father.

我父亲跟你父亲**年纪一样**。Wǒ fùqīn gēn nǐ fùqīn niánjì yīyàng.

Those shoes are **the same price as** these shoes.

那些鞋子和这些鞋子**价格一样**。Nàxiē xiézi hé zhèxiē xiézi jiàgé yīyàng.

My English and your **English level** are **the same**.

你的**英语水平**和我的**一样**。Nǐ de Yīngyǔ shuǐpíng hé wǒ de yīyàng.

Today's **temperature** is **the same as** yesterday's.

今天的**温度**和/跟昨天的**一样**。Jīntiān de wēndù hé/gēn zuótiān de yīyàng.

You write with **the same pen as** me.

你用的**钢笔**跟我的**一样**。Nǐ yòng de gāngbǐ gēn wǒ de yīyàng.

She cooks dinner using **the same utensils as** me.

她做晚饭用的**餐具**跟我用的**一样**。Tā zuò wǎnfàn yòng de cānjù gēn wǒ yòng de yīyàng.

Eating two bowls of noodles is **the same as** eating 3 bowls of rice.

吃两碗面条**等于**吃三碗米饭。Chī liǎng wǎn miàntiáo děngyú chī sān wǎn mǐfàn.

Drinking alcohol is **the same as** drinking poison.

喝酒**等于**喝毒。Hē jiǔ děngyú hē dú.

I am **as clever as** she is/I am **as clever as** her.

我跟她**一样聪明**。Wǒ gēn tā yīyàng cōngmíng.

This tree is **as tall as** those trees.

这棵树跟那些树**一样高**。Zhè kē shù gēn nàxiē shù yīyàng gāo.

I am definitely **as honest as** my elder brother.

我肯定跟我哥哥**一样诚实**。Wǒ kěndìng gēn wǒ gēge yīyàng chéngshí.

Another way to say 'as...as...' (有):

Are you **as clever as** her?

你**有**她**聪明**吗？ Nǐ yǒu tā cōngmíng ma?

Are you **as busy as** your husband?

你**有**你的丈夫**忙**吗？ Nǐ yǒu nǐ de zhàngfū máng ma?

Is that building **as tall as** this one?

那栋建筑**有**这栋建筑**高**吗？ Nà dòng jiànzhú yǒu zhè dòng jiànzhú gāo ma?

Can you play basketball **as well as** me?

你**有**我打篮球打**得好**吗？ Nǐ yǒu wǒ dǎ lánqiú dǎ de hǎo ma?

Can she sing **as well as** you?

她**有**你唱**得好**吗？ Tā yǒu nǐ chàng de hǎo ma?

Does a dog walk **as slowly as** a turtle?

一只狗**有**一只海龟走**得慢**吗？ Yī zhǐ gǒu yǒu yī zhǐ hǎiguī zǒu de màn ma?

When comparing two things that are different from each other:

This watch is **not the same as** that watch.

这款手表跟/和那款手表**不一样**。Zhè kuǎn shǒubiǎo gēn/hé nà kuǎn shǒubiǎo bù yīyàng.

这款手表**不**跟/和那款手表**一样**。Zhè kuǎn shǒubiǎo bù gēn/hé nà kuǎn shǒubiǎo yīyàng.

Those vegetables are **not the same as** these vegetables.

那些蔬菜跟/和这些蔬菜**不一样**。Nàxiē shūcài gēn/hé zhèxiē shūcài bù yīyàng.

那些蔬菜**不**跟/和这些蔬菜**一样**。Nàxiē shūcài bù gēn/hé zhèxiē shūcài yīyàng.

Those vegetables are **not all the same**.

那些蔬菜**不是都一样的**。Nàxiē shūcài bú shì dōu yīyàng de.

These two pencils are **not the same/identical**.

这两支铅笔**不一样**。 Zhè liǎng zhī qiānbǐ bù yīyàng.

It **isn't as hot** today **as** it was yesterday.

今天的天气**不像**昨天**那么热**。Jīntiān de tiānqì bú xiàng zuótiān nàme rè.

今天的天气**不比**昨天的**热**。Jīntiān de tiānqì bù bǐ zuótiān de rè.

This watch is **not as expensive as** that watch.

这款手表**不比**那款手表**贵**。Zhè kuǎn shǒubiǎo bù bǐ nà kuǎn shǒubiǎo guì.

这款手表**不像**那款手表**一样贵**。Zhè kuǎn shǒubiǎo bú xiàng nà kuǎn shǒubiǎo yīyàng guì.

I am **not as clever as** him/he is.

我**没有**他**聪明**。Wǒ méi yǒu tā cōngmíng.

She is **not as patient as** her mother.

她**没有**她母亲**耐心**。Tā méi yǒu tā mǔqīn nàixīn.

They do **not** run **as fast as** the other athletes.

他们**没有**其他的运动员**跑得快**。Tāmen méi yǒu qítā de yùndòngyuán pǎo de kuài.

I **can't write** Chinese **as fast as** Chinese people.

我的中文**没有**中国人**写得快**。Wǒ de Zhōngwén méi yǒu Zhòngguó rén xiě de kuài.

not equal to (不如):

Nobody **is equal to** me.

谁都**不如**我。Shéi dōu bùrú wǒ.

My voice is not **as good as/not equal to** my brother's.

我的嗓子**不如**我哥哥。Wǒ de sǎngzi bùrú wǒ gēge.

Driving is **not as fast as/not as equally fast as** flying.

开车**不如**飞机**快**。Kāichē bùrú fēijī kuài.

quite different (n + 差很多):

They may look the same, but they are **quite different**.

它们也许看起来一样，但是它们**差很多**/完全**不一样**。

Tāmen yěxǔ kànqǐlái yīyàng, dànshì tāmen chà hěn duō/wánquán bù yīyàng.

There's **a large difference between** the cost of a Ferrari and a Ford car.

法拉利和福特汽车的价格**差很多**。

Fǎlālì hé Fútè qìchē de jiàgé chà hěn duō.

The following are examples of expressing doing something 'as + adverb + as' somebody else:

I always **run as fast as** him in a race.

我总是在比赛中跟他**跑得一样快**。Wǒ zǒngshì zài bǐsài zhōng gēn tā pǎo de yīyàng kuài.

Do you need **to eat as much as** him?

你需要跟他**吃得一样多**吗？Nǐ xūyào gēn tā chī de yīyàng duō ma?

I usually **play basketball as often as** my best friend.

我**经常**和最好的朋友一起**打篮球**。Wǒ jīngcháng hé zuìhǎo de péngyǒu yīqǐ dǎ lánqiú.

I never drink **as much alcohol as** he does.

我从不**像**他**喝那么多**的酒。Wǒ cóngbù xiàng tā hē nàme duō de jiǔ.

Does she have **as many days off as** you do?

她和你**一样**休那**么多假**吗？Tā hé nǐ yīyàng xiū nàme duō jiǎ ma?

There are plenty of people who can **teach as well as** me.

有很多人可以**像我一样教学**。Yǒu hěn duō rén kěyǐ xiàng wǒ yīyàng jiàoxué.

I am not sure if/whether they want to **do as much as** me for this project.

我不确定他们是否愿意跟我**一样尽全力做**这个项目。(是否 means 'if/whether')

Wǒ bú quèdìng tāmen shìfǒu yuànyì gēn wǒ yīyàng jìnquánlì zuò zhè gè xiàngmù.

Expressing doing some activity 'not as + adverb + as' somebody else (没有...得 + adv):

I **don't** run **as fast as** she does/her.

我**没有**她跑**得快**。Wǒ méi yǒu tā pǎo de kuài.

I **don't** start **as early as** she does/her.

我**没有**她开始**得早**。Wǒ méi yǒu tā kāishǐ de zǎo.

I **can't/don't** drink **as much beer as** he does/can.

我**没有**他喝**得多**。Wǒ méi yǒu tā hē de duō.

He **doesn't** want to travel **as much as** his wife does.

他**没有**他的妻子旅行**得多**。Tā méi yǒu tā de qīzi lǚxíng de duō.

I **can't** play tennis **as well as** he does/him.

我**没有**他打网球打**得好**。Wǒ méi yǒu tā dǎ wǎngqiú dǎ de hǎo.

He **doesn't** start work **as late as** I do/me.

他**没有**我**那么迟**上班。Tā méi yǒu wǒ nàme chí shàngbān.

My father **doesn't** do **as much housework as** my mother.

我父亲**没有**我母亲做家务做**得多**。Wǒ fùqīn méi yǒu wǒ mǔqīn zuò jiāwù zuò de duō.

Their teacher **doesn't** give his students **as much homework as** he would like.

他们的老师**没有**给学生**足够的作业**。Tāmen de lǎoshī méi yǒu gěi xuéshēng zúgòu de zuòyè.

Unit 50

我姐妹比我用功得多。她比我耐心一点。我的教育程度不如我太太。

美国吉他更贵。我的西装豪华，（但是）你的更豪华。

Unit 51

她比我跑步跑得少。她跑步跑得比我少。我比我最好朋友游泳游得快。

他总是比我穿得更合适。他们比我更有效地完成了工作。

Unit 52

那个房间比这个房间更冷。

他比她更喜欢巧克力。他们比我更快地开展业务。

Unit 53

你的英语水平和我一样。 她做晚饭用的餐具跟我用的一样。

我跟她一样聪明。 你有你的丈夫忙吗？

Unit 54

A 跟/和 + B 不一样； A 不像 B 那么 + adj； A 不 比 B + adj or A 并不像 B 一样 +adj；

A 没有 B + A adj； A 不如 B； A + B + noun 差很多。

Unit 55

我总是在比赛中跟他跑得一样快。

我从不像他喝那么多的酒。有很多人可以像我一样教学。

Unit 56

我没有她跑得快。

我父亲没有我母亲做家务做得多。

These are examples of using superlatives in Mandarin:

In our class he **runs the fastest**.

在我们的班上，他**跑步最快**。Zài wǒmen de bān shàng, tā pǎobù zuì kuài.

Russia is **the largest** county in the world.

在世界上，俄罗斯是**最大的**国家。Zài shìjiè shàng, Éluósī shì zuì dà de guójiā.

Today is **the hottest** day of the year.

今天是今年中**最热的**一天。Jīntiān shì jīnnián zhōng zuì rè de yītiān.

That dress is **the most expensive** one in the shop.

在这家商店，那件连衣裙**最贵**。Zài zhè jiā shāngdiàn, nà jiàn liányīqún zuì guì.

Our house has **the most beautiful** garden in the street.

在这条街上，我们的花园**最漂亮**。Zài zhè tiáo jiē shàng, wǒmen de huāyuán zuì piàoliang.

My son is **the most hardworking** student in his class.

在我儿子班上，我儿子**最努力学习**。Zài wǒ érzi bān shàng, wǒ érzi zuì nǔlì xuéxí.

My husband likes drinking beer **the most**.

我丈夫**最喜欢**喝啤酒。Wǒ zhàngfū zuì xǐhuān hē píjiǔ.

I prefer playing tennis **the most**.

我**最喜欢**打网球。Wǒ zuì xǐhuān dǎ wǎngqiú.

one of the (...最好...之一):

He is **one of the best** students in our whole school.

在这所学校里他是**最好**的学生之一。Zài zhè suǒ xuéxiào lǐ tā shì zuìhǎo de xuéshēng zhīyī.

Crab is **one of my most delicious** types of seafood.

螃蟹是我的**最喜欢吃**的美味海鲜之一。Pángxiè shì wǒ de zuì xǐhuān chī de měiwèi hǎixiān zhīyī.

There are different ways to express either (noun + than + noun + adj + quantity) or (noun + times + adj + noun). The following are examples of (noun + 比 + noun + adj + quantity):

My daughter is **2 years younger than** hers.

我女儿比她的**小两岁**。Wǒ nǚ'ér bǐ tā de xiǎo liǎng suì.

Her son is **four years older than** yours.

她的儿子比你的（儿子）**大四岁**。Tā de érzi bǐ nǐ de (érzi) dà sì suì.

I usually **arrive 10 minutes later than** you.

我通常比你**晚十分钟到达**单位。Wǒ tōngcháng bǐ nǐ wǎn shí fēnzhōng dàodá dānwèi.

My wife always **arrives 15 minutes earlier than** me.

我妻子总是比我**早到达十五分钟**。Wǒ qīzi zǒngshì bǐ wǒ zǎo dàodá shíwǔ fēnzhōng.

I spent **200 yuan more than** I did last time.

我比上次**多花了200元**。Wǒ bǐ shàng cì duō huā le 200 yuán.

You spent **500 yuan less than** I did last time.

你比我上次**少花了500元**。Nǐ bǐ wǒ shàng cì shǎo huā le 500 yuán.

There are **50% more students** at this school this year **compared with** last year.

今年在这个学校的学生人数比去年**多**（增长）**50%**。

Jīnnián zài zhè gè xuéxiào de xuéshēng rénshù bǐ qùnián duō (zēngzhǎng) 50%.

When using (倍) to talk about 'times', it is used differently depending on the structure of the sentence: (是...倍) or (比...倍). When using (比...倍) the (比) adds 1, so (A 比 B 一倍) = twice/two times:

This mobile phone **is twice as expensive/twice** the price as your one.

这款手机的价格**是**你的**两倍**。 Zhè kuǎn shǒujī de jiàgé shì nǐ de liǎng bèi. (是...两倍 = twice)

This mobile phone **is twice as expensive/twice** the price as your one.

这款手机**比**你的手机**贵一倍**。 Zhè kuǎn shǒujī bǐ nǐ de shǒujī guì yī bèi. (比...一倍 = twice)

My homework is **twice as difficult as** yours.

我的作业的难度**是**你**的两倍**。 Wǒ de zuòyè de nándù shì nǐ de liǎng bèi.

These clothes are **twice as expensive as** last year.

这些衣服**比**去年**贵一倍**。 Zhèxiē yīfú bǐ qùnián guì yī bèi.

Edward's mother **drinks 3 times as** much **as** his father.

爱德华妈妈饮酒量是爸爸的三倍。 Àidéhuá māma yǐnjiǔ liàng shì bàba de sān bèi.

This coat is **half the price of** that coat.

这件外套**比**那件外套价格**便宜一半**。 Zhè jiàn wàitào bǐ nà jiàn wàitào jiàgé piányi yībàn.

My bedroom is at least **3 times as big as** my brother's.

我的卧室至少**是**我哥哥的**三倍大**。 Wǒ de wòshì zhìshǎo shì wǒ gēge de sān bèi dà.

I clean the house **3 times as much as** you do.

我打扫房子的次数**是**你的**三倍**。 Wǒ dǎsǎo fángzi de cìshù shì nǐ de sān bèi.

Here is a list of how to use comparative adjectives for both countable and uncountable nouns:

Countable nouns 可数名词	Uncountable nouns 不可数名词
...more...than...比...多	...more...than... 比...多
...the most...最多...	...the most...最多
...fewer...than...比...少	...less...than...比...少
...few... 很少	...little... 很少
...the fewest...最少	...the least...最少

Countable nouns:

I eat **more grapes than** you.

我吃的葡萄**比**你吃得**多**。Wǒ chī de pútáo bǐ nǐ chī de duō.

She eats **the most French fries**.

法式炸薯条她吃**得最多**。Fàshì zhà shǔtiáo tā chī de zuìduō.

她吃的法式炸薯条**最多**。Tā chī de Fàshì zhà shǔtiáo zuìduō.

I drink **fewer cans** of Coke than him.

我喝的可乐罐**比**他**少**。Wǒ hē de Kělè guàn bǐ tā shǎo.

There are **few people** in this restaurant.

这家餐馆的人**很少**。Zhè jiā cānguǎn de rén hěn shǎo.

In our family, I usually eat **the fewest desserts**.

在我家通常我吃甜点吃**得最少**。Zài wǒ jiā tōngcháng wǒ chī tiándiǎn chī de zuìshǎo.

The adverbs 'still', 'yet' and 'already' are used as follows:

I am **still** here. 我**还**在这里。 Wǒ hái zài zhèlǐ.

I am **still** a teacher. 我**还是**一名老师。 Wǒ háishì yī míng lǎoshī.

She is **still** waiting for her parents to come and pick her up from school.

她**仍然**在等她父母来接她放学。 Tā réngrán zài děng tā fùmǔ lái jiē tā fàngxué.

The plane **still** didn't leave after everybody was onboard.

每个人都登机后，飞机**仍然**没有离开。 Měi gè rén dōu dēngjī hòu, fēijī réngrán méi yǒu líkāi.

It is **still** a beautiful place.

这里**依然**是一个漂亮的地方。 Zhèlǐ yīrán shì yī gè piàoliang de dìfāng.

He isn't here **yet**. = He still isn't here.

他**仍然**不在。 Tā réngrán bú zài.

They aren't ready **yet**.

他们**尚未**准备好。 Tāmen shàngwèi zhǔnbèi hǎo.

Don't rush! The film won't start **yet**.

别急，这部电影**还没有**开始。 Bié jí, zhè bù diànyǐng hái méi yǒu kāishǐ.

I am **already** bored with this film.

我**已经**厌倦了这部电影。 Wǒ yǐjīng yànjuàn le zhè bù diànyǐng.

They are **already** on their way to the cinema.

他们**已经**在去电影院的路上了。 Tāmen yǐjīng zài qù diànyǐngyuàn de lù shàng le.

Did she **already** start her new job?

她**已经**开始新工作了吗？ Tā yǐjīng kāishǐ xīn gōngzuò le ma?

When talking about situations that might occur in the future, 'If..., then...' (如果..., 就...) for normal spoken and written Mandarin. The (就) can be omitted:

If it is snowing this evening, I **won't** drive the car.

如果今晚下雪了，我**就**不开车了。Rúguǒ jīnwǎn xiàxuě le, wǒ jiù bù kāichē le.

If the weather changes, **make sure** you bring some extra clothes.

如果天气变化了，**就**请你确保带一些额外的衣服。

Rúguǒ tiānqì biànhuà le, jiù qǐng nǐ quèbǎo dài yīxiē éwài de yīfú.

If you're hungry later, you **can** order some takeaway food.

如果以后一会儿你饿了，**就**可以点一些外卖食品。

Rúguǒ yǐhòu yī huǐr nǐ è le, jiù kěyǐ diǎn yīxiē wàimài shípǐn.

If you take a taxi, it **will be** quicker.

如果你乘坐出租车，这样**会**比较快。Rúguǒ nǐ chéngzuò chūzūchē, zhè yàng huì bǐjiào kuài.

If you go on foot, it **will be** healthier.

如果你走路去，这样**会**比较健康。Rúguǒ nǐ zǒulù qù, zhè yàng huì bǐjiào jiànkāng.

If the weather stays like this, it **will be** a perfect day.

如果天气像这样保持下去，这将**会**是完美的一天。

Rúguǒ tiānqì xiàng zhè yàng bǎochí xiàqù, zhè jiāng huì shì wánměi de yītiān.

If the flight is delayed, **then** what will she do?

如果航班延误了，她**会**怎么做？Rúguǒ hángbān yánwù le, tā huì zěnme zuò?

If she can't buy any tickets for the play, **what can** she do?

如果她买不到这个剧的票，她**能**做什么？

Rúguǒ tā mǎi bú dào zhè gè jù de piào, tā néng zuò shénme?

If Father doesn't want go, **why should** we go?

如果父亲不想去，我们为什么**要**去？Rúguǒ fùqīn bù xiǎng qù, wǒmen wèi shénme yào qù?

What could your boss do **if** you're away from work for too long?

如果你长时间离开工作，你的老板会做什么？

Rúguǒ nǐ cháng shíjiān líkāi gōngzuò, nǐ de lǎobǎn huì zuò shénme?

What will we do **if** we are late for school?

如果我们上学迟到了该怎么办？ Rúguǒ wǒmen shàngxué chídào le gāi zěnme bàn?

Why are there so many chairs here **if** there are only a few guests?

如果只有几个客人，为什么这里有这么多的椅子？

Rúguǒ zhǐ yǒu jǐ gè kèrén, wèi shénme zhèlǐ yǒu zhème duō de yǐzi?

If..., then... (如果...的话, 就...):

If she arrives late, (then) we can eat later.

如果她迟到了**的话**，我们**就**可以晚一点吃饭。

Rúguǒ tā chídào le de huà, wǒmen jiù kěyǐ wǎn yī diǎn chīfàn.

If you win, (then) we can go out and celebrate.

如果你赢了，我们**就**可以在一起出去庆祝。

Rúguǒ nǐ yíng le, wǒmen jiù kěyǐ zài yīqǐ chūqù qìngzhù.

If you come over, (then) I will prepare some snacks.

如果你过来**的话**，那我**就**准备一些小吃。

Rúguǒ nǐ guòlái de huà, nà wǒ jiù zhǔnbèi yīxiē xiǎochī.

You can omit the (如果) and just add (的话) and (就), but (的话) can be omitted:

If it isn't delicious, (then) don't eat it.

不美味**的话**，**就**别吃。Bù měiwèi de huà, jiù bié chī.

If the drink is delicious, (then) drink some more.

饮料好喝**的话**，**就**再喝一些。Yǐnliào hǎo hē de huà, jiù zài hē yīxiē.

If you like the food, just order some more.

你喜欢这个食品，**就**再订购一些。Nǐ xǐhuān zhè gè shípǐn, jiù zài dìnggòu yīxiē.

If..., then... (要是...的话, 就...) or (要是..., 就...) for informal spoken Mandarin:

If you lose, please don't worry.

要是你输了**的话**，请不要担心。Yàoshi nǐ shū le de huà, qǐng bú yào dānxīn.

If I see her, I will discuss the issue with her.

要是我见到她，**就**跟她一起讨论难题。Yàoshi wǒ jiàndào tā, jiù gēn tā yīqǐ tǎolùn nàntí.

If you lie to me, I will know.

要是你对我说谎，我会知道的。Yàoshi nǐ duì wǒ shuōhuǎng, wǒ huì zhīdào de.

For very informal spoken Mandarin, (要我说) can be used:

If you ask me, I wouldn't go.

要我说，我不去。Yào wǒ shuō, wǒ bú qù.

If you ask me, I don't think it's a great idea.

要我说，我认为这不是一个好主意。Yào wǒ shuō, wǒ rènwéi zhè bú shì yī gè hǎo zhǔyì.

If..., then... (假使/假如...的话, 就...) are formal ways used for writing or speeches:

If there is a typhoon tomorrow, **then** we cannot travel.

假使/假如明天有台风**的话**，我们**就**不可以出去旅游了。

Jiǎshǐ/jiǎrú míngtiān yǒu táifēng de huà, wǒmen jiù bù kěyǐ chūqù lǚyóu le.

If he behaves badly again, **then** he might have to be expelled.

假使/假如他再次表现不好，**就**有可能被驱逐了。

Jiǎshǐ/jiǎrú tā zàicì biǎoxiàn bù hǎo, jiù yǒu kěnéng bèi qūzhú le.

If the government's proposal is successful, **then** we will all benefit from the tax cuts.

假使/假如政府的提议成功**的话**，我们所有的人**就会**从减税中获利。Jiǎshǐ/jiǎrú zhèngfǔ de

tíyì chénggōng de huà, wǒmen suǒyǒu de rén jiù huì cóng jiǎn shuì zhōng huòlì.

What if...? In the unlikely event that..., ...? (万一):

What if the teacher doesn't come?

万一老师不来怎么办？Wànyī lǎoshī bù lái zěnme bàn?

Write slowly! **What if** you write a mistake?

写慢点！万一你写错了呢？Xiě màn diǎn! Wànyī nǐ xiěcuò le ne?

What if we cannot get a seat?

万一我们找不到座位怎么办？Wànyī wǒmen zhǎo bú dào zuòwèi zěnme bàn?

Only if... (只有...才...):

Only if you drink less beer will you lose weight easily.

只有少喝啤酒你才能轻松减肥。Zhǐ yǒu shǎo hē píjiǔ nǐ cái néng qīngsōng jiǎnféi.

I believe you can win **only if** you train from dawn till dusk.

我相信只有日以继夜地训练你才能赢。Wǒ xiāngxìn zhǐyǒu rìyǐ jìyè de xùnliàn nǐ cái néng yíng.

Only if you finish work early every day will you have time to do your hobby.

只有每天早一点下班你才有时间从事你的爱好。

Zhǐ yǒu měi tiān zǎo yī diǎn xiàbān nǐ cái yǒu shíjiān cóngshì nǐ de àihào.

If it is not..., (then) it must be... (如果不..., 那...):

If it isn't over there, (then) it must be in the car.

如果不在那边，那它一定在车里。Rúguǒ bú zài nàbiān, nà tā yīdìng zài chē lǐ.

If he isn't working, (then) he's playing golf.

如果不在工作，那他就是在打高尔夫。Rúguǒ bú zài gōngzuò, nà tā jiùshì zài dǎ gāoěrfū.

If he didn't do it, (then) it must have been her.

如果他没有做，那就一定是她。Rúguǒ tā méi yǒu zuò, nà jiù yīdìng shì tā.

When talking about events or situations that are theoretical (second conditional), there is no change to the previous ways of constructing a sentence:

If I **were** you, I **would** enter the competition.

如果我是你**的话**，**就**参加比赛。Rúguǒ wǒ shì nǐ de huà, jiù cānjiā bǐsài.

If I **knew** a way, I **would** tell you.

要是我知道一个办法，**就**告诉你。Yàoshi wǒ zhīdào yī gè bànfǎ, jiù gàosù nǐ.

If the authorities **were** not incompetent, the problem **could** be solved quickly.

假使/假如官方没有无能为力**的话**，难题就能很快得到解决。

Jiǎshǐ/jiǎrú guānfāng méi yǒu wúnéng wéilì de huà, nántí jiù néng hěn kuài de dào jiějué.

For the third conditional, the (了) can be placed at the end of the sentence to show a theoretical change:

If he **had had** enough time, he **could have gone** with you.

(在那时间) **如果**他有足够时间的话，他本可以和你一起去了。

(Zài nà shíjiān) rúguǒ tā yǒu zúgòu shíjiān de huà, tā běn kěyǐ hé nǐ yīqǐ qù le.

If I **had been** there, I **might have been** able to help.

(在那时间) **要是**我去过那里，我**就**可能帮上忙了。

(Zài nà shíjiān) yàoshi wǒ qùguò nàlǐ, wǒ jiù kěnéng bāng shàng máng le.

If I **had known** her anxiety issues, I **would not have disturbed** her.

(在那时间) **假如**我知道她的焦虑问题，**就**不会打扰她了。

(Zài nà shíjiān) jiǎrú wǒ zhīdào tā de jiāolǜ wèntí, jiù bú huì dǎrǎo tā le.

Summary of units 57 – 63

Unit 57

在我们的班上，他跑步最快。在我儿子班上，我儿子最努力学习。

我最喜欢打网球。螃蟹是我的最喜欢吃的美味海鲜之一。

Unit 58

这款手机的价格是你的两倍。(是...两倍 = twice)

这款手机比你的手机贵一倍。(比...一倍 = twice)

Unit 59

我吃的葡萄比你吃得多。我喝的可乐罐数比他少。

在我家通常我吃甜点吃得最少。

Unit 60

我还是一名老师。 别急，这部电影还没有开始。

他们尚未准备好。我已经厌倦了这部电影。

Unit 61

如果...，就...；如果...，会...；如果...的话，...就...；...的话，...就...

要我说...，；假使...，就...；假如...，就...

Unit 62

万一老师不来怎么办？只有少喝啤酒你才能轻松减肥。

如果不在工作，那他就是在打高尔夫。

Unit 63

如果我是你的话，就参加比赛。要是我去过那里，我就可能帮上忙。

（在那时间）如果他有足够时间的话，他本可以和你一起去了。

The following are examples of how to use prepositions in complex sentences:

in （在）里面	on （在）上面	over （在）上面
next to （在）旁边	behind （在）后面	in front of （在）前面
under （在）下面	opposite （在）对面	near/close to （在）附近
far from （在）远离	underneath （下面）	around （围绕）
through/across （穿过）	across/opposite （对面）	between （在...中间）

The new vase is **between** the painting and the photograph.

新花瓶**在**画和照片**之间**。Xīn huāpíng zài huà hé zhàopiàn zhījiān.

Let's take a walk **through** the park.

让我们**在**公园里**散步**吧。Ràng wǒmen zài gōngyuán lǐ sànbù ba.

We should go **across** the road to get to the bank.

我们应该**穿过**马路去那家银行。Wǒmen yīnggāi chuānguò mǎlù qù nà jiā yínháng.

A new shopping centre has opened **opposite** my workplace.

在我工作场所的**对面**开了一家新购物中心。

Zài wǒ gōngzuò chǎngsuǒ de duìmiàn kāi le yī jiā xīn gòuwù zhòngxīn.

There should be some frozen peas **underneath** the ice cream in the freezer.

在冰箱冷藏室的冰淇淋**下面**应该有一些冷冻的豌豆。

Zài bīngxiāng lěngcángshì de bīngqílín xiàmiàn yīnggāi yǒu yīxiē lěngdòng de wāndòu.

I was bored, so I walked **around** the city to find a pub.

我感到无聊，所以我去了城市里**转转**找酒吧。

Wǒ gǎndào wúliáo, suǒyǐ wǒ qù le chéngshì lǐ zhuànzhuàn zhǎo jiǔbā.

We never walk **around** our city at night.

我们晚上从来不**在**我们的城市**周围散步**。

Wǒmen wǎnshàng cónglái bú zài wǒmen de chéngshì zhōuwéi sànbù.

If we stroll **across** the bridge, we can see some beautiful scenery.

如果我们**漫步过**桥，我们可以看到一些美丽的风景。

Rúguǒ wǒmen mànbù guò qiáo, wǒmen kěyǐ kàndào yīxiē měilì de fēngjǐng.

You can sit **between** your two cousins.

你可以**坐在**你两个表哥**之间**。Nǐ kěyǐ zuò zài nǐ liǎng gè biǎogē zhījiān.

I can see it **along** the road.

沿着路，我可以看见它。Yánzhe lù, wǒ kěyǐ kànjiàn tā.

Let's take a stroll **along** this path.

让我们**沿着**这条路漫步/散步。Ràng wǒmen yánzhe zhè tiáo lù mànbù/sànbù.

It is dangerous to run **along** the road at night.

在晚上**沿着**这条路**跑步**是危险的。Zài wǎnshàng yánzhe zhè tiáo lù pǎobù shì wēixiǎn de.

I looked **through** the window and saw them arguing.

我**透过**窗户看到了他们在争吵。Wǒ tòuguò chuānghù kàndào le tāmen zài zhēngchǎo.

I used to live **far from** the big city.

我曾经住**在远离**大城市的地方。Wǒ céngjīng zhù zài yuǎnlí dà chéngshì de dìfāng.

among (当中):

I am the best **among** all my colleagues.

我是所有同事**当中**最好的一个。Wǒ shì suǒyǒu tóngshì dāngzhōng zuìhǎo de yī gè.

Among all my friends, you are my favourite.

你是我所有的朋友**当中**最喜欢的一个。Nǐ shì wǒ suǒyǒu de péngyǒu dāngzhōng zuì xǐhuān de yī gè.

among the aforementioned (其中):

I have had three wives. **Of all of them**, Sara was the happiest.

我曾经有三个妻子，**其中**萨拉是最高兴的。

Wǒ céngjīng yǒu sān gè qīzi, qízhōng Sàlā shì zuì gāoxìng de.

I have also got 3 sons. **Of all of them**, Peter is the cleverest.

我也有三个儿子，**其中**彼得是最聪明的。

Wǒ yě yǒu sān gè érzi, qízhōng Bǐdé shì zuì cōngmíng de.

within (在...内...):

I usually finish my homework **within** 20 minutes.

我通常**在**二十分钟**内**写完作业。Wǒ tōngcháng zài èrshí fēnzhōng nèi xiěwán zuòyè.

It is impossible for you to do it **within** a week.

你不可能**在**一个星期**内**做好。Nǐ bù kěnéng zài yī gè xīngqī nèi zuòhǎo.

including (包括...在内...):

Including you, our group consists of five people.

包括你**在内**，我们的团队由五个人组成。(由...组成 means 'consists of')

Bāokuò nǐ zài nèi, wǒmen de tuánduì yóu wǔ gè rén zǔchéng.

I have already read many books, **including** your ones.

我已经看过很多书了，**包括**你的书**在内**。

Wǒ yǐjīng kànguò hěn duō shū le, bāokuò nǐ de shū zài nèi.

It is time **to have** dinner.

是时候吃晚饭了。Shì shíhòu chī wǎnfàn le.

It is time **to get back** home.

是时候回家了。Shì shíhòu huíjiā le.

It is time **to start** preparing lunch for the family.

是时候开始为家人准备午饭了。Shì shíhòu kāishǐ wèi jiārén zhǔnbèi wǔfàn le.

It is time **to redecorate** this entire house.

是时候重新装修整个房子了。Shì shíhòu chóngxīn zhuāngxiū zhěng gè fángzi le.

It is time **for you** to stop playing with your computer.

是时候停止玩电脑了。Shì shíhòu tíngzhǐ wán diànnǎo le.

It is time **for me** to tell you about him.

是时候告诉你关于他的事了。Shì shíhòu gàosù nǐ guānyú tā de shì le.

It is time **for us** to go home.

现在是我们回家的时候了。Xiànzài shì wǒmen huíjiā de shíhòu le.

It is time **for your parents** to help you find a decent high school.

现在是你父母帮助你找一所体面高中的时候了。

Xiànzài shì nǐ fùmǔ bāngzhù nǐ zhǎo yī suǒ tǐmiàn gāozhōng de shíhòu le.

It is getting late. It is time **we went** home.

时间不早了，是时候回家了。Shíjiān bù zǎo le, shì shíhòu huíjiā le.

It is time **they stopped** wasting time playing cards.

他们是时候停止浪费时间打扑克牌了。Tāmen shì shíhòu tíngzhǐ làngfèi shíjiān dǎ pūkèpái le.

It is time **I painted** the living-room again.

是时候重新给卧室刷墙了。Shì shíhòu chóngxīn gěi wòshì shuā qiáng le.

It is time **he bought** some new clothes.

他该买一些新衣服了。Tā gāi mǎi yīxiē xīn yīfú le.

It is normal to prefer something over something else. Here are examples of how to express (prefer + noun + to another noun) and (prefer + gerund + to another gerund):

I **prefer** this jacket **to** that one.

跟那件夹克**比**，我**更喜欢**这件。(跟…比 means 'prefer…to')

Gēn nà jiàn jiákè bǐ, wǒ gèng xǐhuān zhè jiàn.

I **prefer** these jeans **to** those trousers.

跟那件裤子**比**，我**更喜欢**这件牛仔裤。

Gēn nà jiàn kùzi bǐ, wǒ gèng xǐhuān zhè jiàn niúzǎikù.

I **prefer** those classical cars **to** these modern cars.

与那些现代的汽车**比**，我**更喜欢**那些古典的汽车。(与…比 also means 'prefer…to')

Yǔ nàxiē xiàndài de qìchē bǐ, wǒ gèng xǐhuān nàxiē gǔdiǎn de qìchē.

She **prefers** driv**ing** her car **to** walk**ing**.

跟散步**比**，她**更喜欢**开（她的）车。

Gēn sànbù bǐ, tā gèng xǐhuān kāi tā de chē.

They **prefer** exercis**ing** in a gym to exercis**ing** at home.

跟在家锻炼**比**，他们**更喜欢**在健身房锻炼。

Gēn zài jiā duànliàn bǐ, tāmen gèng xǐhuān zài jiànshēnfáng duànliàn.

Sara definitely **prefers** sing**ing** songs **to** danc**ing**.

跟跳舞相**比**，萨拉绝对**更喜欢**唱歌。

Gēn tiàowǔ xiāng bǐ, Sàlā juéduì gèng xǐhuān chànggē.

I prefer A to B (更喜欢 + A, 而不是 B); I would rather...than... (宁愿 A, 而不是 B):

I **prefer to** eat at home **rather than** eat in a restaurant.

我**更喜欢**在家吃饭，**而不是**去餐馆吃饭。

Wǒ gèng xǐhuān zài jiā chīfàn, ér bú shì qù cānguǎn chīfàn.

We all **prefer to** travel to Asia **rather than** Europe.

我们都**更喜欢**去亚洲旅游，**而不是**欧洲。

Wǒmen dōu gèng xǐhuān qù Yàzhōu lǚyóu, ér bú shì Ōuzhōu.

Susan certainly **prefers to** drive quickly **rather than** slowly.

苏珊当然**更喜欢**开快车，**而不是**开慢车。

Sūshān dāngrán gèng xǐhuān kāi kuài chē, ér bú shì kāi màn chē.

I **would rather** stay at home **than** go out tonight.

我今晚**宁愿**待在家里，**而不是**愿意出去。

Wǒ jīnwǎn nìngyuàn dāi zài jiā lǐ, yě bú yuànyì chūqù.

The children **would rather** play computer games **than** board games.

孩子们**宁愿**玩电脑游戏，**而不是**棋盘游戏。

Háizimen nìngyuàn wán diànnǎo yóuxì, ér bú shì qípán yóuxì.

Peter **would rather** work in an office **than** outside.

皮特**宁愿**在办公室工作，**而不是**在外面工作。

Pítè nìngyuàn zài bàngōngshì gōngzuò, ér bú shì zài wàimiàn gōngzuò.

It is useful to talk about a number being more or less the number that is shown (左右):

About 100,000. 十万**左右**。Shí wàn zuǒyòu.

There are **around** 2,000 students in grade 7.

七年级有两千**左右**学生。Qī niánjí yǒu liǎng qiān zuǒyòu xuéshēng.

Sometimes an amount is either what is shown or more than what is shown (之上) or (以上):

The house must be worth **250,000 or more**.

房子肯定价值250,000**之上**。Fángzi kěndìng jiàzhí 250,000 zhīshàng.

I would say that there are **100 or more** people here tonight.

我想说今晚有100或**以上**的人在这里。 Wǒ xiǎng shuō jīnwǎn yǒu 100 huò yǐshàng de rén zài zhèlǐ.

The amount might simply be more than what is shown (多):

There are **more than 60 students** in that classroom.

那间教室里有**六十多**个学生。Nà jiān jiàoshì lǐ yǒu liùshí duō gè xuéshēng.

More than 7,000,000 people live and work in London.

超过七百多万人口在伦敦生活和工作。

Chāoguò qībǎi duō wàn rénkǒu zài Lúndūn shēnghuó hé gōngzuò.

less than (不超过) or (以下):

There are **45 students or fewer** in each class.

每个班级里有**不超过**四十五个学生。Měi gè bānjí lǐ yǒu bù chāoguò sìshíwǔ gè xuéshēng.

That old car **is worth 2,500 or less**.

那辆汽车价值在**两千五百以下**。Nà liàng qìchē jiàzhí zài liǎng qiān wǔbǎi yǐxià.

The amount could be 'less than' something (不到 or 以下); almost (差不多 or 大约) some amount:

Is the price **less than** 80%?

价格**不到**百分之八十吗？Jiàgé bú dào bǎi fēn zhī bāshí ma?

I won't sell my car for **less than** 2,000.

2000**以下**我不会卖我的汽车。2000 yǐxià wǒ bú huì mài wǒ de qìchē.

Surely that house costs **less than** 500,000.

当然那所房子价格**不到**50万。Dāngrán nà suǒ fángzi jiàgé bú dào 50 wàn.

There could **almost** be 7,000,000 people living in London.

伦敦可能有**差不多**七百万人居住。Lúndūn kěnéng yǒu chàbuduō qībǎi wàn rén jūzhù.

There are **almost** 50 students in the swimming pool.

游泳池里有**差不多**五十个学生。Yóuyǒngchí lǐ yǒu chàbuduō wǔshí gè xuéshēng.

I can **almost** see 15 cars along this street.

沿着这条街我能看到**大约**十五辆车。Yánzhe zhè tiáo jiē wǒ néng kàndào dàyuē shíwǔ liàng chē.

An indeterminate amount of anything is something people often use when they do not know exactly what the amount should or is going to be:

I might be back in **3 or 4 days**.

我可能**三四天**回来。Wǒ kěnéng sān-sì tiān huílái.

It could cost you **50 – 75 yuan** to buy a new wing-mirror.

你可能需要花**五十到七十五块**钱买新后视镜。

Nǐ kěnéng xūyào huā wǔshí dào qīshíwǔ kuài qián mǎi xīn hòushìjìng.

It could take **5-6 years** before we can complete the project.

我们有可能会用**五六年**完成这个工程。

Wǒmen yǒu kěnéng huì yòng wǔ-liù nián wánchéng zhè gè gōngchéng.

Temperatures (温度):

Today's temperature is 25 **degrees Celsius**.

今天的温度是25摄氏度。Jīntiān de wēndù shì 25 shèshìdù.

Last winter the temperature was minus 10 **degrees Celsius**.

去年的冬天温度是零下10摄氏度。Qùnián de dōngtiān wēndù shì língxià 10 shèshìdù.

It's raining now. 现在下雨了。Xiànzài xiàyǔ le.

It's very windy today. 今天风很大。Jīntiān fēng hěn dà.

If the discount is 20% off the original price, you can see an advertisement saying 80% or 8 折.

This means 20% of the original price:

30 percent off – 7折 qī zhé   50 percent off – 五折 wǔ zhé   75 percent off – 2.5 折 èr diǎn wǔ zhé

It might be useful, especially in business or science, to ask and answer questions about materials:

What is this **made of**? 这是什么做的？ Zhè shì shénme zuò de?

This is **made of** metal. 这个是用金属做的。Zhè gè shì yòng jīnshǔ zuò de.

What is this table **made of**? 这张桌子是用什么做的？ Zhè zhāng zhuōzi shì yòng shénme zuò de?

The table is **made of wood**. 这张桌子是用木头做的。Zhè zhāng zhuōzi shì yòng mùtóu zuò de.

What are your shoes **made of**? 你的鞋子是用什么做的？ Nǐ de xiézi shì yòng shénme zuò de?

My shoes are **made from** plastic and rubber. 我的鞋子是用塑料和橡胶做的。Wǒ de xiézi shì yòng sùliào hé xiàngjiāo zuò de.

leather 皮革 pígé	wood 木头 mùtóu	glass 玻璃 bōli
cotton 棉花 miánhuā	plastic 塑料 sùliào	diamond 钻石 zuànshí
nylon 尼龙 nílóng	metal 金属 jīnshǔ	fur 皮毛 pímáo
silk 丝绸 sīchóu	wool 羊毛 yángmáo	gold 黄金 huángjīn

each other (互相) or (彼此):

The children were usually glad to play with **each other**.

孩子们通常乐意**互相**玩耍。Háizimen tōngcháng lèyì hùxiāng wánshuǎ.

We saw **each other** outside the theatre.

我们在剧院外看到了**对方**。Wǒmen zài jùyuàn wài kàndào le duìfāng.

We often teach **each other** to do different things.

我们经常**互相**教导做不同的事。Wǒmen jīngcháng hùxiāng jiàodǎo zuò bùtóng de shì.

They are very kind to **each other**.

他们**彼此**很友好。Tāmen bǐcǐ hěn yǒuhǎo.

We always try to help **each other**.

我们总是尝试**彼此**帮助。Wǒmen zǒngshì chángshì bǐcǐ bāngzhù.

I think it's best that we pretend that we like **each other**.

我认为最好我们假装**彼此**喜欢。Wǒ rènwéi zuìhǎo wǒmen jiǎzhuāng bǐcǐ xǐhuān.

together (在一起):

We often enjoy playing **together**.

我们经常喜欢**在一起**玩。Wǒmen jīngcháng xǐhuān zài yīqǐ wán.

They would sometimes go into the forest **together** to find wood for the fire.

他们有时会**在一起**去森林里寻找木柴。Tāmen yǒushí huì zài yīqǐ qù sēnlín lǐ xúnzhǎo mùchái.

It is hard to get them to stick **together** perfectly.

很难让它们完美地结合**在一起**。Hěn nán ràng tāmen wánměi de jiéhé zài yīqǐ.

Together we are stronger.

我们**在一起**，更强大。Wǒmen zài yīqǐ, gèng qiángdà.

Unit 64

让我们在公园里散步吧。在冰箱冷藏室的冰淇淋下面应该有一些冷冻的豌豆。

让我们沿着这条路漫步/散步。

Unit 65

我是所有同事当中最好的一个。我有过三个妻子，其中萨拉是最高兴的。

我已经看过很多书了，包括你的书在内。

Unit 66

是时候吃晚饭了。现在是我们回家的时候了。

是时候重新给卧室刷墙了。

Unit 67

跟那裤子比，我更喜欢这牛仔裤。跟散步比，她更喜欢开车。

我们都更喜欢去亚洲旅游，而不是欧洲。皮特宁愿在办公室工作，而不是在外面工作。

Unit 68

about: number + 左右；below: number + 以下；above: number + 之上/以上 number + 多；

less than: 不到 + number；almost: 差不多/大约 + number 3 or 4 days: 三四天

Unit 69

今天的温度是25摄氏度。7折这是什么做的？

这张桌子是用什么做的？这张桌子是用木头做的。

Unit 70

孩子们通常乐意互相玩耍。

我们总是尝试彼此帮助。我们在一起，更强大。

In Mandarin 'other' (其他的) is used for one or more than one thing or person:

There are **other** things to do.

还有**其他的**事情要做。Hái yǒu qítā de shìqíng yào zuò.

Don't worry! There will be **other** chances to do it better.

别担心！还有**其他的**机会去把它做得更好。

Bié dānxīn, hái yǒu qítā de jīhuì qù bǎ tā zuò de gènghǎo.

I have **other** questions that I want to ask you.

我有**其他的**问题要问你。Wǒ yǒu qítā de wèntí yào wèn nǐ.

Do you know any **other** reasons why it broke?

你知道它破了的**其他的**原因吗？Nǐ zhīdào tā pò le de qítā de yuányīn ma?

another (另一个) is used for one thing or person:

I know **another** person who can speak 5 languages.

我认识**另一个**人，他能说5种语言。Wǒ rènshi lìng yī gè rén, tā néng shuō 5 zhǒng yǔyán.

There is **another** way of collecting information quickly.

有**另一种快速**收集资料的方法。Yǒu lìng yī zhǒng kuàisù shōují zīliào de fāngfǎ.

Can you think of **another** place where we can get some olive oil?

你能想到**另一个**我们能买到一些橄榄油的地方吗？

Nǐ néng xiǎngdào lìng yī gè wǒmen néng mǎidào yīxiē gǎnlǎn yóu de dìfāng ma?

I count 5 chairs, but there should be **another** chair for Aunt Doreen.

我数了有5把椅子，但是应该还有**另一把**给多琳阿姨的椅子。

Wǒ shù le yǒu 5 bǎ yǐzi, dànshì yīnggāi hái yǒu lìng yī bǎ gěi Duōlín āyí de yǐzi.

There is no distinction between 'each' and 'every' in Mandarin:

Each story book was interesting. (Each book in the group of books)

每本故事书都很有趣。（故事书中的每本书）

Měi běn gùshì shū dōu hěn yǒuqù. (Gùshì shū zhōng de měi běn shū)

Each player in the team was excited. (Each one in the team)

每个球员都很兴奋。（团队中的每一个）

Měi gè qiúyuán dōu hěn xīngfèn. (Tuánduì zhōng de měi yī gè)

Can you tell me what **each** one cost, please?

你能告诉我每个费用吗？Nǐ néng gàosù wǒ měi gè fèiyòng ma?

Every magazine was boring. (Every magazine in the group)

每本杂志都很无聊。（小组中的每本杂志）

Měi běn zázhì dōu hěn wúliáo. (Xiǎozǔ zhōng de měi běn zázhì)

Every city in China is unique. (All the cities in China)

中国的每座城市都是独特的。（中国所有城市）

Zhōngguó de měi zuò chéngshì dōu shì dútè de. (Zhōngguó suǒyǒu chéngshì)

I will consider **every** possible solution.

我会考虑每一个可能的解决方案。Wǒ huì kǎolǜ měi yī gè kěnéng de jiějué fāng'àn.

I go to work at 7:30 a.m. **every day**.

我**每天**早上7点半去上班。

Wǒ **měi tiān** zǎoshàng 7 diǎn bàn qù shàngbān.

The church bells ring **every hour**.

教堂的钟声**每个**小时都会响起。

Jiàotáng de zhōngshēng **měi gè** xiǎoshí dōu huì xiǎngqǐ.

Everyone in the class was glad to finish early.

班上的**每个人**都很高兴能早点完成。

Bān shàng de **měi gè rén** dōu hěn gāoxìng néng zǎo diǎn wánchéng.

I knew almost **everyone** at the dinner party.

在晚宴上的**所有人**我几乎都认识。Zài wǎnyàn shàng de **suǒyǒu rén** wǒ jīhū dōu rènshi.

I like the mugs because **every one/each one** was a different colour.

我喜欢这些杯子，因为**每一个**都是不同的颜色。

Wǒ xǐhuān zhèxiē bēizi, yīnwèi **měi yī gè** dōu shì bùtóng de yánsè.

I hate celebrations, but I must go to **every one/each one every** year.

我讨厌庆祝活动，但是**每**年我必须**每一场**都去。

Wǒ tǎoyàn qìngzhù huódòng, dànshì **měi** nián wǒ bìxū **měi yī chǎng** dōu qù.

Every person here is hardworking.

每个人都努力工作。

Měi gè rén dōu nǔlì gōngzuò.

Everyone enjoys strolling along the park.

谁都享受在公园里散步。

Shéi dōu xiǎngshòu zài gōngyuán lǐ sànbù.

No one thinks it's a good idea.

谁都不认为是一个好主意。Shéi dōu bú rènwéi shì yī gè hǎo zhǔyì.

I finish work late **every** day.

我**天天**晚下班。

Wǒ tiāntiān wǎn xiàbān.

It is busy **everywhere** today.

今天**哪里都**很忙。

Jīntiān nǎlǐ dōu hěn máng.

When talking about the future, it is useful to say that some activity will start only after another is/has finished:

I **will** start preparing dinner **when** I get home.

我回家**后会**开始准备晚餐。Wǒ huíjiā hòu huì kāishǐ zhǔnbèi wǎncān.

Jane **will** come to our house **when** she has got some free time.

当她有空闲时间**时**，简**会**来我们家。Dāng tā yǒu kòngxián shíjiān shí, Jiǎn huì lái wǒmen jiā.

Father **will** definitely repair the garden fence **when** summer arrives.

夏天到来**时**，父亲肯定**会**修理花园围栏。Xiàtiān dàolái shí, fùqīn kěndìng huì xiūlǐ huāyuán wéilán.

I think I **will** start planting new flowers **when** the sun comes out.

太阳出来**的时候**，我想我**会**种新花。Tàiyáng chūlái de shíhòu, wǒ xiǎng wǒ huì zhòng xīn huā.

When the school term is over, we **will** all go on a nice trip together.

学期结束**后**，我们**将**一起去旅行。

Xuéqī jiéshù hòu, wǒmen jiāng yīqǐ qù lǚxíng.

When your grandmother is feeling better, **she'll** visit us.

当你的祖母感觉好些**时**，她**会**拜访我们。

Dāng nǐ de zǔmǔ gǎnjué hǎoxiē shí, tā huì bàifǎng wǒmen.

When Christmas is here, we **will** start enjoying more delicious foods.

当圣诞节来临**时**，我们**会**开始享受更多美味的食物。(来临时 means 'comes/arrives')

Dāng Shèngdànjié láilín shí, wǒmen huì kāishǐ xiǎngshòu gèngduō měiwèi de shíwù.

When your mother arrives, we **will** tell her the good news.

你妈妈回来**的时候**，我们**会**告诉她好消息。

Nǐ māma huílái de shíhòu, wǒmen huì gàosù tā hǎo xiāoxī.

I **will** get some groceries **after** I finish work.

我完成工作**后会**收到一些杂货。Wǒ wánchéng gōngzuò hòu huì shōudào yīxiē záhuò.

The Petersons **will** have a house party **before** we get back from holiday.

在我们从假期回来**以前**，彼得森一家**将**举行家庭聚会。

Zài wǒmen cóng jiàqī huílái yǐqián, Bǐdésēn yījiā jiāng jǔxíng jiātíng jùhuì.

She **will** study extra classes **while** she is at college.

她**在**大学**期间会**学习额外的课程。Tā zài dàxué qījiān huì xuéxí éwài de kèchéng.

They **won't** start **until** we arrive.

他们**不会**在我们到达**以前**开始。Tāmen bú huì zài wǒmen dàodá yǐqián kāishǐ.

We **will** go out for a walk **if** the weather is suitable.

如果天气适宜，我们**会**出去散步。Rúguǒ tiānqì shìyí, wǒmen huì chūqù sànbù.

Another way to say 'when' (等..., 会...) or (等到...后, 会...):

When the boss finds out, we **will** be fired.

等到老板知道**后**，我们**会**被解雇的。Děngdào lǎobǎn zhīdào hòu, wǒmen huì bèi jiěgù de.

When the typhoon stops, I **will** do some shopping.

等到台风停了，我**会**出去买东西。Děngdào táifēng tíng le, wǒ huì chūqù mǎi dōngxī.

When one activity must lead to another, or they are both strongly related:

When travelling in China, **it will always** involve seeing many scenic spots and eating many dishes.

在中国旅行**时**，**总少**不了看很多风景名胜和吃很多菜。

Zài Zhōngguó lǚxíng shí, zǒngshǎo bùliǎo kàn hěn duō fēngjǐng míngshèng hé chī hěn duō cài.

When there's a birthday party, **there's always** alcohol and many guests.

有生日聚会**的时候**少不了酒和很多客人。

Yǒu shēngrì jùhuì de shíhòu shǎo bùliǎo jiǔ hé hěn duō kèrén.

on time (准时):

I always arrive at school **on time**.

我总是**准时**到学校。 Wǒ zǒngshì zhǔnshí dào xuéxiào.

The plane took off **on time**.

飞机**准时起**飞了。 Fēijī zhǔnshí qǐfēi le.

Please don't be late. Be **on time**!

请你不要迟到。要**准时**！ Qǐng nǐ bú yào chídào. Yào zhǔnshí!

in time (及时):

She went to work **in time** to go to the meeting.

她**及时**上班去参加会议。

Tā jíshí shàngbān qù cānjiā huìyì.

I hope you can be here **in time** to say goodbye to your grandparents.

我希望你能**及时**赶到这里和爷爷奶奶说再见。

Wǒ xīwàng nǐ néng jíshí gǎndào zhèlǐ hé yéye nǎinai shuō zàijiàn.

My father is often late, so he **never** arrives **in time** for dinner.

我父亲经常迟到，所以吃晚饭他**从来不及时**赶到。

Wǒ fùqīn jīngcháng chídào, suǒyǐ chī wǎnfàn tā cónglái bù jíshí gǎndào.

just in time (及时):

I **managed to finish** the race **just in time**.

我设法**及时**完成比赛了。

Wǒ shèfǎ jíshí wánchéng bǐsài le.

Luckily, I **arrived home just in time** to watch the start of the football match.

幸运的是，我**及时**到家观看了足球比赛的开场。

Xìngyùn de shì, wǒ jíshí dào jiā guānkàn le zúqiú bǐsài de kāichǎng.

These are examples of talking about approximate times of when activities start or finish:

At the beginning of term, the students are always excited.

在学期**开始的时候**，学生都总是很兴奋。

Zài xuéqī kāishǐ de shíhòu, xuéshēng dōu zǒngshì hěn xīngfèn.

Chinese people have a holiday **at the beginning of** Spring Festival.

在春节**开始的时候**，中国人会放假。Zài Chūnjié kāishǐ de shíhòu, Zhōngguó rén huì fàngjià.

At first, I hated my new workplace, but **in the end** my colleagues were all great.

起初，我讨厌我的新工作场所，但是最后我的同事都很棒了。

Qǐchū, wǒ tǎoyàn wǒ de xīn gōngzuò chǎngsuǒ, dànshì zuìhòu wǒ de tóngshì dōu hěn bang le.

In the middle of June, we will start a new course.

在六月**中旬**，我们将开始我们的新课程。

Zài liù yuè zhōngxún, wǒmen jiāng kāishǐ wǒmen de xīn kèchéng.

Just before the end of the year, you will have time to relax.

就在年底前，你会有时间放松一下。Jiù zài nián dǐqián, nǐ huì yǒu shíjiān fàngsōng yīxià.

In the end/finally, I had to quit my job.

最后，我不得不辞掉了工作。Zuìhòu, wǒ bùdé bù cídiào le gōngzuò.

At the end of the night, we all went back home.

在深夜，我们都回到家了。Zài shēnyè, wǒmen dōu huídào jiā le.

At the end of January, you should be able to speak Chinese.

一月**底**，你应该会说中文了。Yīyuè dǐ, nǐ yīnggāi huì shuō Zhōngwén le.

Unfortunately, we arrived **at the end of** the movie.

不幸的是，我们在电影**结束时**才到。Búxìng de shì, wǒmen zài diànyǐng jiéshù shí cái dào.

The movie was so boring that **in the end/finally** we left the cinema early.

电影相当无聊，**最后**我们提早离开电影院了。

Diànyǐng xiāngdāng wúliáo, zuìhòu wǒmen tízǎo líkāi diànyǐngyuàn le.

Just like in English, there are intensifiers that can add additional meaning to an adverb or adjective.

(这么) is used if the person or thing is nearby; (那么) is used of it or the person is somewhere else.

so + adverb: ˋ

He runs **so quickly**. 他跑得**这么**快。Tā pǎo de zhème kuài.

She speaks **so slowly**. 她说得**这么**慢。Tā shuō de zhème màn.

They walked **so quietly**. 他们走得**那么**安静了。Tāmen zǒu de nàme ānjìng le.

I never wake up **so early**. 我从来不**这么**早醒来过。Wǒ cónglái bú zhème zǎo xǐnglái guò.

so + adjective:

Those boys are **so clever**. 那些男孩子**真**聪明。Nàxiē nán háizi zhēn cōngmíng.

Those girls are **so athletic**. 那些女孩子都**真**运动。Nàxiē nǔ háizi dōu zhēn yùndòng.

He has been in there for **so long**. 他在那里已经**很长时间**了。Tā zài nàlǐ yǐjīng hěn cháng shíjiān le.

This watch is **so expensive**. 这款手表**如此之**贵。Zhè kuǎn shǒubiǎo rúcǐ zhī guì.

such + noun:

I don't like **such people**. 我不喜欢**这些人**。Wǒ bù xǐhuān zhèxiē rén.

I prefer **such foods**. 我更喜欢**这些食物**。Wǒ gèng xǐhuān zhèxiē shíwù.

He is **such** a handsome **man**. 他是一个**如此**英俊的男人。Tā shì yī gè rúcǐ yīngjùn de nánrén.

She is **such** an honest **woman**. 她是一个**如此**诚实的女人。Tā shì yī gè rúcǐ chéngshí de nǔrén.

I waited **such a long time**. 我等了**这么**久。Wǒ děng le zhème jiǔ.

I have been reading this novel **for ages**. 我已经读了这本小说**很久**了。Wǒ yǐjīng dú le zhè běn xiǎoshuō

hěn jiǔ le.

Unit 71

还有其他的事情要做。

有另一种快速收集资料的方法。

Unit 72

每个球员都很兴奋。

中国的每个城市都是独特的。

Unit 73

班上的每个人都很高兴能早点完成。

我讨厌庆祝活动，但是每年我必须每一场都去。

Unit 74

我...时，...会...；我...的时候，...会...；当...时，...会...；...后会...；不会...之前...；

等到...后，...会...；...时，...总少不了...

Unit 75

飞机准时起飞了。她及时上班去参加会议。

我设法及时完成比赛了。

Unit 76

...开始的时候，...；...起初；...中旬，...

就在年地前，...；最后...，；...低

Unit 77

她说得那么/这么慢。那些男孩真聪明。

我不喜欢这些人。 他是个如此英俊的男人。

In Mandarin there is no such thing as a 'perfect tense' in the sense that native English speakers understand it. Here are some examples of how to say 'perfect simple' and 'past simple' tenses:

I have been busy today.	I **was** busy today.
我今天很忙。Wǒ jīntiān hěn máng.	我今天很忙。Wǒ jīntiān hěn máng.
She has lost her car keys tonight.	She **lost** her car keys tonight.
她今晚**丢了**车钥匙。Tā jīnwǎn diū le chē yàoshi.	她今晚**丢了**车钥匙。Tā jīnwǎn diū le chē yàoshi.
It has stopped raining this week.	It **stopped** raining this week.
这周雨停了。Zhè zhōu yǔ tíng le.	这周雨停了。Zhè zhōu yǔ tíng le.

As is shown, there is no difference between the 'perfect simple' and 'past simple'. However, there are ways of making 'present perfect simple' sentences when using 'already' (已经), 'just' (刚才), 'yet' (还没有) and expressing a past experience that happened some time ago (过):

They **have eaten** today.

今天他们**已经**吃了。Jīntiān tāmen yǐjīng chī le. (了 goes after verb or verb phrase)

I **have already** visited my grandparents this week.

我这周**已经**去看爷爷奶奶了。Wǒ zhè zhōu yǐjīng qù kàn yéye nǎinai le.

I **have already** read those story books.

我**已经**看了那些故事书。Wǒ yǐjīng kàn le nàxiē gùshì shū.

I **have just** finished my homework.

我**刚刚**做完作业了。 Wǒ gānggang zuòwán zuòyè le. (了 goes after verb or verb phrase)

He **has just** come home.

他**刚才**回家了。Tā gāngcái huíjiā le.

Derek **has just** called his boss.

德里克**刚才**打电话给他的老板了。Délǐkè gāngcái dǎ diànhuà gěi tā de lǎobǎn le.

They **haven't prepared** dinner **yet**.

他们**还没有**准备晚饭。Tāmen hái méi yǒu zhǔnbèi wǎnfàn.

I **haven't started** my school project **yet**.

我**还没有**开始我学校的项目。Wǒ hái méi yǒu kāishǐ wǒ xuéxiào de xiàngmù.

I **haven't been** to Singapore **yet**.

我**还没有**去过新加坡。 Wǒ hái méi yǒu qùguò Xīnjiāpō.

(过 goes immediately after the verb to show completion or no completion in the past)

I **have been** to Shanghai.

我**去过**上海。Wǒ qùguò Shànghǎi.

I **have ridden** a horse many times.

我**骑过**很多次马。Wǒ qíguò hěn duō cì mǎ.

I **have never eaten** caviar.

我**还没有吃过**鱼子酱。Wǒ hái méi yǒu chīguò yúzǐjiàng.

'been' and 'gone' are as follows:

I **have been** to the bank.

我**去过**银行了。Wǒ qùguò yínháng le. (The 去过 means 'been')

I **have been** to many cities in China.

我在中国**去过**很多城市了。Wǒ zài Zhōngguó qùguò hěn duō chéngshì le.

Father **has gone** to the bank. (He's still there now)

我父亲**去**银行了。Wǒ fùqīn qù yínháng le.   (The 去了 means 'gone')

I think Sara **has gone** to bed.

我想萨拉**去**睡觉了。Wǒ xiǎng Sàlā qù shuìjiào le.

Making questions in present perfect simple:

Have you **been** to Brazil?

你去过巴西吗？ Nǐ qùguò Bāxī ma?

Have you **drunk** Scotch whiskey?

你喝过苏格兰威士忌吗？ Nǐ hēguò Sūgélán wēishìjì ma?

Have you already seen her new house?

你已经看过他的新房子了吗？ Nǐ yǐjīng kànguò tā de xīn fángzi le ma?

Have you **eaten**? 你吃饭了吗？ Nǐ chīfàn le ma?

你吃了没有？ Nǐ chī le méi yǒu?

Has she arrived in Shanghai **yet**? 她到上海了吗？ Tā dào Shànghǎi le ma?

Have they finished their lunch **yet**? 他们吃午饭了吗？ Tāmen chī wǔfàn le ma?

How have you been recently? 你最近怎么样了？ Nǐ zuìjìn zěnme yàng le?

ever (曾经):

Have you **ever been** to Peru? 你曾经去过秘鲁吗？ Nǐ céngjīng qùguò Bìlǔ ma?

Yes, I have been to Peru before. 是的，我以前去过秘鲁。 Shì de, wǒ yǐqián qùguò Bìlǔ.

No, I have **never been** to Peru. 不，我从没有去过秘鲁。 Bù, wǒ cóng méi yǒu qùguò Bìlǔ.

Have you **ever** eaten uncooked crab?

你曾经吃过未经烹煮的螃蟹吗？ Nǐ céngjīng chīguò wèijīng pēngzhǔ de pángxiè ma?

Yes, I **have eaten** uncooked crab before.

是的，我以前吃过未经烹煮的螃蟹。 Shì de, wǒ yǐqián chīguò wèijīng pēngzhǔ de pángxiè.

No, I **have never eaten** uncooked crab.

不，我以前从没有吃过未经烹煮的螃蟹。 Bù, wǒ yǐqián cóng méi yǒu chīguò wèijīng pēngzhǔ de pángxiè.

When asking about 'How long...?' something has occurred, the answer can use either 'since' or 'for' as follows:

How long have you lived in this city?

你住在这座城市多久了？ Nǐ zhù zài zhè zuò chéngshì duōjiǔ le?

I have lived in this city **for** 5 years.

我在这座城市住了五年。 Wǒ zài zhè zuò chéngshì zhù le wǔ nián.

How long have you been a student?

你成为学生多久了？ Nǐ chéngwéi xuéshēng duōjiǔ le?

I have been a student **for** 7 years.

我成为学生七年了。Wǒ chéngwéi xuéshēng qī nián le.

since:

How long have you lived/been living in this city?

你在这座城市住了多久了？ Nǐ zài zhè zuò chéngshì zhù le duōjiǔ le?

I have lived/been living in this city **since** 2015.

我从2015年住在这座城市了。Wǒ cóng 2015 nián zhù zài zhè zuò chéngshì le.

How long have you been a student?

你成为学生多久了？ Nǐ chéngwéi xuéshēng duōjiǔ le?

I have been a student **since** 2013.

我从2013年开始成为一名学生。Wǒ cóng 2013 nián kāishǐ chéngwéi yī míng xuéshēng.

I have been busy **since** the beginning of this year.

年初**以来**，我都很忙。Nián chū yǐlái, wǒ dōu hěn máng.

Since starting work, I have had more money to spend.

自从开始工作**以来**，我已经花了很多钱。Zìcóng kāishǐ gōngzuò yǐlái, wǒ yǐjīng huā le hěn duō qián.

Here are more examples of making questions in Mandarin using the perfect simple tense:

How have you been **since** you started learning Chinese?

自从你开始学习中文**以来**，你过得怎么样？

Zìcóng nǐ kāishǐ xuéxí Zhōngwén yǐlái, nǐ guòdé zěnme yàng?

How many new friends have you made **since** moving to a new city?

自从搬新城市**以来**，你**交**过多少新朋友？

Zìcóng bān xīn chéngshì yǐlái, nǐ jiāoguò duōshǎo xīn péngyǒu?

Ever since I left England, I have felt happier.

自从我离开英格兰**以来**，我感到更快乐。

Zìcóng wǒ líkāi Yīnggélán yǐlái, wǒ gǎndào gèng kuàilè.

Even since I started to learn Chinese, my job prospects have increased markedly.

自从我开始学习中文**以来**，我的就业前景也明显增加。

Zìcóng wǒ kāishǐ xuéxí Zhōngwén yǐlái, wǒ de jiùyè qiánjǐng yě míngxiǎn zēngjiā.

Here are examples of using separable verbs with present perfect tense. The (过...了) indicates

that it happened quite some time ago:

Has he divorced **yet**? 他**离过婚**吗？ Tā lí guò hūn ma?

Yes, he has already got divorced.

是的，他离过婚了。Shì de, tā lí guò hūn le.

Have you ever run a marathon?

你曾经**跑过步**一个马拉松吗？Nǐ céngjīng pǎo guò bù yī gè mǎlāsōng ma?

Yes, I have run a marathon before.

是的，我以前**跑过步**一届马拉松了。Shì de, wǒ yǐqián pǎo guò bù yī jiè mǎlāsōng le.

It is possible to use the (了) aspect particle twice in a sentence. For present perfect simple tense, the additional (了) is used to specify that something is more than what you would expect/have expected, or that the number has the potential to increase in the future.

When the number is more than you expected/have expected:

My friend's friend already has 5 daughters and one son. (More than what you expected)

我朋友的朋友已经**生**了五个女儿和一个儿子了。

Wǒ péngyǒu de péngyǒu yǐjīng sheng le wǔ gè nǚ'ér hé yī gè erzi le.

I cannot believe that you have already drunk 2 bottles of wine.

我不能相信你已经**喝**了两瓶葡萄酒了。

Wǒ bù néng xiāngxìn nǐ yǐjīng hē le liǎng píng pútáojiǔ le.

When you expect the number to be more in the future:

He has already read over/more than 50 books this year.

他今**年看**了多于五十本书了。

Tā jīnnián kàn le duōyú wǔshí běn shū le.

Linda is extremely clever. She has already studied 4 degrees.

琳达挺聪明的，她**已经**学习了四个学位了。

Líndá tǐng cōngmíng de, tā yǐjīng xuéxí le sì gè xuéwèi le.

It is possible to talk about something that has been happening for some time, and now it may or may not be finished. (一直在) is used to say 'up until now' and is going to finish fairly soon:

I have eaten my dinner. 我已经吃过晚饭了。Wǒ yǐjīng chīguò wǎnfàn le. (completed)

I have been eating my dinner. 我一直在吃晚饭。Wǒ yīzhí zài chī wǎnfàn. (not yet completed)

I have cooked dinner.	She **has been cooking** dinner.
我已经做好晚饭了。	她一直在做晚饭。
Wǒ yǐjīng zuòhǎo wǎnfàn le.	Tā yīzhí zài zuò wǎnfàn.
I **have done** my homework.	I **have been doing** my homework.
我已经完成做作业了。	我一直在做作业。
Wǒ yǐjīng wánchéng zuò zuoyè le.	Wǒ yīzhí zài zuò zuoyè.
I **have run** this evening.	I **have been running** all morning.
我今晚已经跑步了。	我一整早上一直在跑步。
Wǒ jīnwǎn yǐjīng pǎobù le.	Wǒ yīzhěng zǎoshàng yīzhí zài pǎobù.

If an activity is ongoing, (了...了) is used:

She has been swimming for 2 hours.

她已经游泳游了两个小时了。Tā yǐjīng yóuyǒng yóu le liǎng gè xiǎoshí le.

I have been studying Chinese since 2004.

我自从2004年就开始学习了中文了。Wǒ zìcóng 2004 nián jiù kāishǐ xuéxí le Zhōngwén le.

I have been teaching English for 12 years.

我已经教了英语十二年了。Wǒ yǐjīng jiào le Yīngyǔ shí'èr nián le.

She **has been** chatting for 3 hours.

她聊天聊了三个小时了。Tā liáotiān liáo le sān gè xiǎoshí le.

Have you been waiting for long? (Activity has just finished)

你已经等很久了吗？ Nǐ yǐjīng děng hěn jiǔ le ma?

Have you been studying hard **since** you were young?

从小到大，你一直在努力学习吗？ Cóng xiǎo dào dà, nǐ yīzhí zài nǔlì xuéxí ma?

What have you been doing? (Recently and up to now, but not including now)

你一直在做什么？ Nǐ yīzhí zài zuò shénme?

What have you been doing **recently**? (Recently and up to now, but not including now)

你最近一直在做什么呢？ Nǐ zuìjìn yīzhí zài zuò shénme ne?

How long have you been waiting for the bus? (Ongoing activity)

你等公共汽车等了多久了？ Nǐ děng gōnggòng qìchē děng le duōjiǔ le?

How long have you been living in Greece? (Ongoing activity)

你在希腊住了多长时间了？ Nǐ zài Xīlà zhù le duōcháng shíjiān le?

How many weeks have you been studying Spanish? (Ongoing activity)

你学习了西班牙语多少个星期了？ Nǐ xuéxí le Xībānyá yǔ duōshǎo gè xīngqī le?

How many years have you been teaching? (Ongoing activity)

你教了多少年了？ Nǐ jiào le duōshǎo nián le?

How often have you been testing this product? (Recently stopped/completed activity)

你多久测试一次这个产品？ Nǐ duōjiǔ cèshì yī cì zhè gè chǎnpǐn?

How often has she been feeling sick?

她多久一次感到恶心？ Tā duō jiǔ yī cì gǎndào ěxīn? (No need to separate verb and adjective)

Again, there is no such tense in Mandarin, so all that is needed is to indicate that the events took place in the past, and that one of them (past perfect tense) took place before the other events:

I **arrived** at her house, but she had **already gone out**.

我**到**了她家，但她**已经出去**了。

Wǒ **dào** le tā jiā, dàn tā **yǐjīng chūqù** le.

I **had sent** her an email, but she **never replied**.

我给她**发过**一封电子邮件，但她**从没有回复**。

Wǒ gěi tā **fāguò** yī fēng diànzǐ yóujiàn, dàn tā **cóng méi yǒu huífù**.

I **had already prepared** lunch when my other relatives **arrived**.

我**已经准备**中饭了的时候我其他的亲戚**到**了。

Wǒ **yǐjīng zhǔnbèi** zhōngfàn le de shíhou wǒ qítā de qīnqi **dào** le.

Since I **had learned** a lot about business, I **was able to get** a suitable job.

因为我**学过**很多方式做生意，我**设法获得**合适的工作。

Yīnwèi wǒ **xuéguò** hěn duō fāngshì zuò shēngyì, wǒ **shèfǎ huòdé** héshì de gōngzuò.

The delivery man **had delivered** our parcel, but we **didn't hear** him ring the doorbell.

送货员**把**我们的包裹送**到**了，但我们**没有**听到他按门铃。

Sònghuò yuán **bǎ** wǒmen de bāoguǒ sòng**dào** le, dàn wǒmen **méi yǒu** tīngdào tā ànménlíng.

I went to bed **after** my parents **had gone** to bed.

我父母去了睡觉以后，我去睡觉了。

Wǒ fùmǔ qù le shuìjiào yǐhòu, wǒ qù shuìjiào le.

I arrived 20 minutes **after** they **had been** waiting for me.

在他们等了我20分钟后，我到了。

Zài tāmen děng le wǒ 20 fēnzhōng hòu, wǒ dào le.

Tim arrived **after** Eric **had** already **gone** home.

提姆到了家以后，埃里克已经回家了

Tímǔ dào le jiā yǐhòu, Āilǐkè yǐjīng huíjiā le.

Before I came to China, I **had** already **travelled** to many different countries.

我来中国以前，我已经旅行去很多其他的国家了。

Wǒ lái Zhōngguó yǐqián, wǒ yǐjīng lǚxíng qù hěn duō qítā de guójiā le.

Father **had** always **wanted** to be a doctor **before** he became an architect.

父亲在成为一名建筑师以前，一直想要成为一名医生。

Fùqīn zài chéngwéi yī míng jiànzhù shī yǐqián, yīzhí xiǎngyào chéngwéi yī míng yīshēng.

I **had had** a large breakfast, **then** I went to work quickly.

我吃完了很大一份早餐，就马上去上班了。

Wǒ chīwán le hěn dà yī fèn zǎocān, jiù mǎshàng qù shàngbān le.

Using the past perfect continuous tense is the same as the past perfect simple, except the activities are those that took some time, and not activities that were conducted quickly:

I **had been/already been waiting** for Sara for 40 minutes **before** she arrived.

在萨拉到达以前我已经等她四十分钟了。

Zài Sàlā dàodá yǐqián wǒ yǐjīng děng tā sìshí fēnzhōng le.

There **had been many people strolling** along the streets **before** the heavy rain came.

在大雨来临以前，曾有很多人在街上闲逛了。

Zài dàyǔ láilín yǐqián, céng yǒu hěn duō rén zài jiē shàng xiánguàng le.

I left the house quickly **after she had been arguing** with her mother for hours.

在她与她母亲持续争吵数小时以后，我迅速离开了这所房子。

Zài tā yǔ tā mǔqīn chíxù zhēngchǎo shù xiǎoshí yǐhòu, wǒ xùnsù líkāi le zhè suǒ fángzi.

I **had been spending** so much time at the library, so I was only then able to get a good degree.

我在图书馆花了这么多时间，直到那以后我才获得了好学位。

Wǒ zài túshūguǎn huā le zhème duō shíjiān, zhídào nà yǐhòu wǒ cái huòdé le hào xuéwèi.

Starting from (从 + time/date + 起,...):

Starting from next year, we will be busier.

从明年**起**，我们将更忙。Cóng míngnián qǐ, wǒmen jiāng gèng máng.

Starting from next week, you have to start earlier.

从下周**起**，你们不得不早一点开始。Cóng xiàzhōu qǐ, nǐmen bùdé bù zǎo yī diǎn kāishǐ.

Since (从 + time/date + 开始/以来):

Since last year, I have met many great people.

从去年**以来**，我遇到过很多伟大的人。Cóng qùnián yǐlái, wǒ yùdào guò hěn duō wěidà de rén.

Since I got married, my wife has given birth to four children.

从我结婚了**以来**，我太太**生了**四个孩子。Cóng wǒ jiéhūn le yǐlái, wǒ tàitai sheng le sì gè háizi.

Since..., in that case... (既然..., 那就...):

Since you don't want to work, **in that case** you can clean the car.

既然你不想工作，**那就**清洁汽车。Jìrán nǐ bù xiǎng gōngzuò, nà jiù qīngjié qìchē.

Since Paul got divorced from his wife, **it is okay** for him to look for a new girlfriend.

既然保罗跟他太太离婚了，**那就**可以找一个新女朋友。

Jìrán Bǎoluó gēn tā tàitài líhūn le, nà jiù kěyǐ zhǎo yī gè xīn nǚ péngyǒu.

Ever since (从...以来) or (自从...以来):

Ever since I started working here, I have learnt many things.

从**我在**这里开始工作**以来**，我**学到了**很多东西。

Cóng wǒ zài zhèlǐ kāishǐ gōngzuò yǐlái, wǒ xuédào le hěn duō dōngxī.

Ever since I was a child, I have been dreaming of the perfect life.

从小**以来**，我一直**梦想拥有**完美的生活。

Cóng xiǎo yǐlái, wǒ yīzhí mèngxiǎng yǒngyǒu wánměi de shēnghuó.

In some circumstances, you might wish to talk about something being completed at some point in the future.

(到 + time/date + pronoun + 将 + verb + 了):

I will have worked/been working here for five years **by next year**.

到**明年**我**将**在这里工作满五年了。

Dào míngnián wǒ jiāng zài zhèlǐ gōngzuò mǎn wǔ nián le.

They will have been studying at university for 2 months **by the end of the week**.

到这个周末他们**将**在大学学习满两个月**了**。

Dào zhè gè zhōumò tāmen jiāng zài dàxué xuéxí mǎn liǎng gè yuè le.

We will have finished this class at 8:00 p.m. tonight.

到**今晚八点**时我**已经**结束这堂课了。

Dào jīnwǎn bā diǎn shí wǒmen yǐjīng jiéshù zhè tángkè le.

Sue will have started her new business by now.

现在苏**已经**开始了她的新业务。

Xiànzài Sū yǐjīng kāishǐ le tā de xīn yèwù.

Will you have been living here for 5 years **by next year**?

到**明年**你**将**在这里住满五年了吗?

Dào míngnián nǐ jiāng zài zhèlǐ zhù mǎn wǔ nián le ma?

Will they have been back home **by now**?

到**现在为止**,他们回到家了吗?

Dào xiànzài wéizhǐ tāmen huídào jiā le ma?

There is no such thing as 'future continuous tense' in Mandarin, so it is only necessary to talk about an activity occurring in the future:

I **will be visiting** my grandparents tomorrow.

我明天**将会拜访**我的祖父母。Wǒ míngtiān jiāng huì bàifǎng wǒ de zǔfùmǔ.

My colleagues **will be having** an important meeting later today.

我的同事都今天晚些时候**将会有**一个重要的会议。(晚些时候 means 'later today')

Wǒ de tóngshì dōu jīntiān wǎn xiē shíhòu jiāng huì yǒu yī gè zhòngyào de huìyì.

She says she **will be doing** more maths homework from now.

她说她从现在开始要做更多的数学作业。

Tā shuō tā cóng xiànzài kāishǐ yào zuò gèngduō de shùxué zuòyè.

I **won't be living** in this city much longer.

我**不会再住**在这座城市了。Wǒ bú huì zài zhù zài zhè zuò chéngshì le.

They **won't be spending** too much time in the library.

他们**不会花**太多了时间在图书馆了。Tāmen bú huì huā tài duō le shíjiān zài túshū guǎn le.

My cousin, Louise, **won't be travelling** with us next summer holiday.

我的表弟，路易斯下个暑假**不会**跟我们一起**旅游**了。

Wǒ de biǎodì, Lùyìsī xià gè shǔjià bú huì gēn wǒmen yīqǐ lǚyóu le.

Will their teachers **be giving** them extra classes before the tests?

他们的老师**会**在考试前给他们额外的补习课吗？

Tāmen de lǎoshī huì zài kǎoshì qián gěi tāmen éwài de bǔxí kè ma?

Will David **be selling** his favourite things when he moves to a new house?

大卫搬到新房子时，**会**卖掉他最喜欢的东西吗？

Dàwèi bāndào xīn fángzi shí, huì màidiào tā zuì xǐhuān de dōngxī ma?

Unit 78

今天他们已经吃了。 他刚才回家了。他们还没有准备晚饭。我去过上海。

你成为学生多久了？ 我不能相信你已经喝了两瓶葡萄酒了。

Unit 79

我一直在吃晚饭。我自从2004年就开始学习了中文了。

你已经等很久了吗？

Unit 80

我给她发过一封电子邮件，但她从没有回复。

父亲在成为一名建筑师之前，一直想要成为一名医生。

Unit 81

我在图书馆花了这么多时间，直到那以后我才获得了好学位。

Unit 82

从明年起，我们将更忙。从去年以来，我遇到过很多伟大的人。

从我在这里开始工作以来，我学到了很多东西。

Unit 83

到今晚八点时我们已经结束这堂课了。

到明年你将在这里住满五年了吗？

Unit 84

我明天将会拜访我的祖父母。

我不会再住在这个城市了。

It is sometimes problematic to keep writing 'who' or 'what' did the action given by the verb. Sometimes we want to focus on what happened, not 'who' or 'what' did it:

My living-room table **is made of** wood. (made of = one material)

我起居室的桌子是用木头**做的**。Wǒ qǐjūshì de zhuōzi shì yòng mùtóu zuò de.

That ornament **is made from** gold and silver. (made from = 2 or more materials)

那件装饰品是用金银**制成的**。Nà jiàn zhuāngshìpǐn shì yòng jīnyín zhìchéng de.

In passive voice (被), the object goes at the beginning of the sentence:

The football was kicked **by** him. 足球是**被**他踢的。Zúqiú shì bèi tā tī de.

He was shot 3 times. 他**被**枪击了三次。Tā bèi qiāngjī le sān cì.

She was seen many times. 她**被**看到过很多次。Tā bèi kàndào guò hěn duō cì.

All the seafood was eaten **by** her. 所有的海鲜都**被**她吃了。Suǒyǒu de hǎixiān dōu bèi tā chī le.

The criminal was arrested **by** the police. 罪犯**被**警察逮捕了。Zuìfàn bèi jǐngchá dàibǔ le.

The negative forms of passive voice sentences just take the usual form:

He wasn't shot 3 times.

他**没有被**枪击三次。Tā méi yǒu bèi qiāngjī sān cì.

She wasn't seen many times.

她**没有被**看到很多次。Tā méi yǒu bèi kàndào hěn duō cì.

None of the seafood was eaten **by** her.

没有海鲜是被她吃掉的。Méi yǒu hǎixiān shì bèi tā chī diào de.

她**没有吃**任何海鲜。Tā méi yǒu chī rènhé hǎixiān.

The criminal wasn't arrested **by** the police. (There needs to be something after the verb_)

罪犯**没有被**警察逮捕。Zuìfàn méi yǒu bèi jǐngchá dàibǔ. or 没有罪犯是**被**警察逮捕**的**。

It is important to remember that not all sentences can be changed into passive voice; you can only use transitive verbs. For example, to see, to kick, to eat, to drink, to play, to hit. You cannot use 'to swim, to feel, or to like':

Simple tenses:

I see her. = She **is** seen **by** me.

我看见她。Wǒ kànjiàn tā. = 她**被**我看到。Tā bèi wǒ kàndào.

I kicked the ball. = The ball **was** kicked **by** me.

我踢了那个球。Wǒ tī le nà gè qiú. = 那个球**被**我踢了。Nà gè qiú bèi wǒ tī le.

I will meet her tomorrow. = She **will be** met **by** me tomorrow.

我明天要见她。Wǒ míngtiān yào jiàn tā. = 她明天会**被**我约见。Tā míngtiān huì bèi wǒ yuējiàn.

Continuous tenses:

I am eating dinner. = Dinner **is being** eaten **by** me.

我正在吃晚饭。Wǒ zhèngzài chī wǎnfàn. = 晚饭正在**被**我吃。Wǎnfàn zhèngzài bèi wǒ chī.

They were playing football. = Football **was being** played **by** them.

他们踢足球了。Tāmen tī zúqiú le. = 足球**被**他们踢了。Zúqiú bèi tāmen tī le.

She will be lecturing students next week. = Students **will be being** lectured **by** her next week.

她将会在下周给学生都讲课。Tā jiānghuì zài xià zhōu gěi xuéshēng dōu jiǎngkè. =

她的学生都将会在下周**由**她讲课。Tā de xuéshēng dōu jiānghuì zài xià zhōu yóu tā jiǎngkè.

Perfect tenses:

I have read this book. = This book **has been** read **by** me.

我已经看过这本书了。Wǒ yǐjīng kànguò zhè běn shū le.

这本书**被**我看了。Zhè běn shū bèi wǒ kàn le.

I had forgotten about the time. = The time **had been** forgotten **by** me.

在那时间，我忘记了时间。Zài nà shíjiān, wǒ wàngjì le shíjiān. =

在那时间，时间**被**我忘记了。Zài nà shíjiān, shíjiān bèi wǒ wàngjì le.

If you want to emphasise a person or thing, then (就是) is used:

You're **exactly** the kind of student I like.

你**就是**我喜欢的那种学生。Nǐ jiùshì wǒ xǐhuān de nà zhǒng xuéshēng.

That man is **just** crazy.

那个男人**就是**疯了。Nà gè nánrén jiùshì fēng le.

only because (只是因为)

I didn't eat more **only because** I had already eaten.

我没吃更多**只是因为**我已经吃饭了。

Wǒ méi chī gèngduō zhǐshì yīnwèi wǒ yǐjīng chīfàn le.

Is Sara entering the competition **just because** it is easy?

萨拉参加比赛**只是因为**它容易吗？Sàlā cānjiā bǐsài zhǐshì yīnwèi tā róngyì ma?

You can use (反正) to show emphasis:

Anyway **I think** everybody knows about his problem.

反正我**想**大家都知道他的问题。Fǎnzhèng wǒ xiǎng dàjiā dōu zhīdào tā de wèntí.

Anyway **it is okay** not to want to go to university.

反正对上大学不感兴趣（也）是可以的。

Fǎnzhèng duì shàng dàxué bù gǎn xìngqù (yě) shì kěyǐ de.

(由) can be used to emphasis the one who performs the action given by the verb:

He is responsible for the broken window.

打破的窗户**由**他**负责**。Dǎpò de chuānghù yóu tā fùzé.

This Chinese class is being **taught by me**.

这节中文课**由**我来**教**。Zhè jié Zhōngwén kè yóu wǒ lái jiào.

Possibilities in the present (可能) and in the past (本可能) or (本可以):

Present and future possibility:

My mother **could be** at home **now**.

我母亲现在**可能**在家了。Wǒ mǔqīn xiànzài kěnéng zài jiā le. (The 了 indicates possible change)

He **could be** angry **right now**.

他现在**可能**在生气了。Tā xiànzài kěnéng zài shēngqì le.

We **could go** to the cinema **tonight**.

我们今晚**可以**去看电影。Wǒmen jīnwǎn kěyǐ qù kàn diànyǐng.

I **could** see her clearly **yesterday**.

我昨天**能**清楚地看到她。Wǒ zuótiān néng qīngchǔ de kàndào tā.

I **couldn't** go shopping because I **was** busy.

我以前**不能**去购物，因为我很忙。Wǒ yǐqián bù néng qù gòuwù, yīnwèi wǒ hěn máng.

The (了) indicates a theoretical change:

My mother **could have been** at home yesterday afternoon.

我妈妈昨天下午**可能**在家里了。Wǒ māma zuótiān xiàwǔ kěnéng zài jiā lǐ le.

We **could have gone** to the cinema. (but, in fact, we didn't)

我们**本可以**去看电影了。（但实际上我们没有）

Wǒmen běn kěyǐ qù kàn diànyǐng le. (Dàn shíjì shàng wǒmen méi yǒu)

He **could have been** angry.

他**本可能**在生气了。Tā běn kěnéng zài shēngqì le.

Exaggerate a feeling (可以 + verb/adjective):

I am so hungry that I **could** eat a horse.

我饿得**可以**吃下一匹马。 Wǒ è de kěyǐ chī xià yī pǐ mǎ.

She says she is so healthy that she **could** swim around the world.

她说她健康得**可以**游泳环游世界。 Tā shuō tā jiànkāng de kěyǐ yóuyǒng huányóu shìjiè.

When talking about a past event that could not have been any more or less than it was, use (不能再...了). The (再...了) means 'anymore', please see unit 139.

They **couldn't have been** kinder to me.

那时候，他们**不能再**对我更好了。 Nà shíhòu, tāmen bù néng zài duì wǒ gènghǎo le.

I **couldn't have eaten** any more seafood.

那时候，我**不能再**吃更多的海鲜了。 Nà shíhòu, wǒ bù néng zài chī gèngduō de hǎixiān le.

Using 'should' (应该) in the present and past:

You **should go** to school earlier today.

你今天**应该**早点**去**上学。Nǐ jīntiān yīnggāi zǎo diǎn qù shàngxué.

You **should have gone** to school earlier yesterday morning.

你昨天早上**应该**早点**去**学校。Nǐ zuótiān zǎoshàng yīnggāi zǎo diǎn qù xuéxiào.

They **should know** not to do that.

他们**应该知道**不要那样做。Tāmen yīnggāi zhīdào bú yào nà yàng zuò.

They **should have known** not to do that.

他们**应该**已经**知道**了不要那样做。Tāmen yīnggāi yǐjīng zhīdào le bú yào nà yàng zuò.

You **shouldn't do** that dangerous activity.

你**不应该做**那种危险的活动。

Nǐ bù yīnggāi zuò nà zhǒng wēixiǎn de huódòng.

You **shouldn't have done** that dangerous activity.

那时候，你**不应该做**那种危险的活动。

Nà shíhòu, Nǐ bù yīnggāi zuò nà zhǒng wēixiǎn de huódòng。

Paul **shouldn't be** so impatient with his students.

保罗**不应该**对他的学生如此不耐烦。

Bǎoluó bù yīnggāi duì tā de xuéshēng rúcǐ bú nàifán.

Paul **shouldn't have been** so impatient with his students.

那时候，保罗**不应该**对他的学生如此不耐烦。

Nà shíhòu, Bǎoluó bù yīnggāi duì tā de xuéshēng rúcǐ bú nàifán。

When talking about something that you personally believe should or shouldn't be, use 'must' (必须). When talking about something that should be, but it is out of your control or many people also agree, use 'have to' (不得不):

You **must** wear some accessories with that dress.

你**必须**穿戴一些配饰来配那条裙子。Nǐ bìxū chuāndài yīxiē pèishì láipèi nà tiáo qúnzi.

You **have to** go to school from Monday to Friday.

你**不得不**从周一到周五去学校。Nǐ bùdé bù cóng zhōuyī dào zhōuwǔ qù xuéxiào.

You **don't have to** go to work tomorrow.

你明天**不必**去上班。Nǐ míngtiān búbì qù shàngbān.

In the past:

You **had to have worn** accessories with that dress.

过去你**必须**穿戴一些配饰来配那件连衣裙。

Guòqù nǐ bìxū chuāndài yīxiē pèishì láipèi nà jiàn liányīqún.

You **had to have gone** to school from Monday to Friday.

过去你**必须**从周一到周五去学校。

Guòqù nǐ bìxū cóng zhōuyī dào zhōuwǔ qù xuéxiào.

He **mustn't have been** so busy when Christmas came.

当圣诞节到来时，他一定**不可能**那么忙。(到来时 means 'upon arrival/arrive')

Dāng Shèngdànjié dàolái shí, tā yīdìng bù kěnéng nàme máng.

When expressing an opinion that somebody 'should' do something, use (需要):

You **need to eat** more vegetables.

你需要多吃蔬菜。Nǐ xūyào duō chī shūcài.

You **needed to have eaten** more vegetables.

在那时间，你需要吃了更多的蔬菜。Zài nà shíjiān, nǐ xūyào chī le gèngduō de shūcài.

Ed **needs to spend** more time working on his project.

爱德华需要花更多的时间在他的项目上。

Àidéhuá xūyào huā gèngduō de shíjiān zài tā de xiàngmù shàng.

Ed **needed to have spent** more time on his project.

(在那时) 爱德华需要花费更多的时间在他的项目上。

(Zài nà shí) Àidéhuá xūyào huāfèi gèngduō de shíjiān zài tā de xiàngmù shàng.

You **needn't/don't need to go** tonight. 你今晚不需要去。Nǐ jīnwǎn bù xūyào qù.

You **needn't have gone**. 你当时没必要去。Nǐ dāngshí méi bìyào qù. (当时 means 'at that time')

She **needn't/doesn't need to wear** that warm coat on this sunny day.

在这样的晴天，她**不需要**穿那件保暖的外套。

Zài zhèyàng de qíngtiān, tā bù xūyào chuān nà jiàn bǎonuǎn de wàitào.

She **needn't have worn** that warm coat on that sunny day.

在那个晴天，她**没必要**穿那件保暖的外套。

Zài nà gè qíngtiān, tā méi bìyào chuān nà jiàn bǎonuǎn de wàitào.

When talking about present and future possibilities, use (可能):

He **may be/might be** sick because he isn't at work.

他可能生病了，因为他不在上班。

Tā kěnéng shēngbìng le, yīnwèi tā bú zài shàngbān.

They **may be/might be** at work because it's already 9:30 a.m.

他们可能在上班了，因为现在已经上午9点半了。

Tāmen kěnéng zài shàngbān le, yīnwèi xiànzài yǐjīng shàngwǔ 9 diǎn bàn le.

Sue **may/might** go to that new department store next week.

苏可能下周去了那家新百货商店。

Sū kěnéng xià zhōu qù le nà jiā xīn bǎihuò shāngdiàn.

She **may/might** eat more food than she should.

她可能吃了过多的食物。

Tā kěnéng chī le guò duō de shíwù.

I **may not/might not** see her if I am busy.

如果我很忙，我可能不会看到她。

Rúguǒ wǒ hěn máng, wǒ kěnéng bú huì kàndào tā.

They **may not/might not** be home this week.

本周他们可能不在家。

Běn zhōu tāmen kěnéng bú zài jiā.

Unit 85

足球是被他踢的。他没有被枪击三次。

晚饭正在被我吃。她的学生都将会在下周由她讲课。

Unit 86

你就是我喜欢的那种学生。我没吃更多只是因为我已经吃过饭了。

反正我想大家都知道他的问题。打破的窗户由他负责。

Unit 87

我母亲现在可能在家了。 我昨天能清楚地看到她。

我妈妈昨天下午可能在家里。 我饿得可以吃下一匹马。

Unit 88

你今天应该早点去上学。

他们应该已经知道了不要那样做。

Unit 89

在那时间，你必须穿戴一些配饰来配那条裙子。

你不得不从周一到周五去学校。 过去你必须从周一到周五去学校。

Unit 90

你需要多吃蔬菜。过去爱德华需要花费更多的时间在他的项目上。

如果你不想，你可以不需要留在这里。

Unit 91

他可能生病了，因为他不在上班。

如果我很忙，我可能不会看到她。

When talking about possibilities in the past, use (可能...了):

He **may have been/might have been** sick because he wasn't at work.

他**可能**已经生病**了**，因为他没在工作。Tā kěnéng yǐjīng shēngbìng le, yīnwèi tā méi zài gōngzuò.

They **may have been/might have been** at work because it was already 9:30 a.m.

他们**可能**在工作**了**，因为现在已经是上午9:30了。

Tāmen kěnéng zài gōngzuò le, yīnwèi xiànzài yǐjīng shì shàngwǔ 9:30 le.

Sue **may have been/might have gone** to that new department store last week.

上周，苏**可能**已经去了那家新百货商店。

Shàng zhōu, Sū kěnéng yǐjīng qù le nà jiā xīn bǎihuò shāngdiàn.

She **may have eaten/might have eaten** more than she should have.

她**可能**吃了比她应该吃得多。Tā kěnéng chī le bǐ tā yīnggāi chī de duō.

I **may not have seen/might not have seen** her if I had been busy.

如果我一直很忙，我**可能没**见过她。Rúguǒ wǒ yīzhí hěn máng, wǒ kěnéng méi jiànguò tā.

They **may not have been/might not have been** at home that week.

那个星期他们**可能没**在家。Nà gè xīngqī tāmen kěnéng méi zài jiā.

Tracey **may not have been/might not have been** with Eric at the bar.

特雷西**可能没**跟埃里克在酒吧。Tèléixī kěnéng méi gēn Āilǐkè zài jiǔbā.

Ben **may not have been/might not have been** preparing his speech all day.

本**可能**一整天都**没**准备他的演讲。Běn kěnéng yī zhěng tiān dōu méi zhǔnbèi tā de yǎnjiǎng.

You might find it useful to talk about what something or somebody does:

A doctor is someone **who** helps sick people get better.

医生是帮助病人变好（恢复健康）的人。

Yīshēng shì bāngzhù bìngrén biànhǎo (huīfù jiànkāng) de rén.

A teacher is someone **who** teaches people new information.

教师是教授人们新知识的人。Jiàoshī shì jiàoshòu rénmen xīn zhīshì de rén.

A supermarket is a place **where** people can buy any kind of food.

超市是人们可以买到任何食物的地方。Chāoshì shì rénmen kěyǐ mǎidào rènhé shíwù de dìfāng.

A theme park is a place **where** people can go to have some fun.

主题公园是人们可以玩乐的地方。Zhǔtí gōngyuán shì rénmen kěyǐ wánlè de dìfāng.

Christmas is a time **when** people get together and have a large family dinner.

圣诞节是人们聚在一起吃家庭晚餐的时刻。

Shèngdànjié shì rénmen jù zài yīqǐ chī jiātíng wǎncān de shíkè.

The Dragon Boat Festival is a time **when** people come together to watch Dragon Boat races and

eat rice dumplings. 端午节是人们聚在一起观看赛龙舟和吃粽子的时刻。

Duānwǔjié shì rénmen jù zài yīqǐ guānkàn sài lóngzhōu hé chī zòngzi de shíkè.

A boss is someone **whose** employees work for him or her.

老板是雇佣他人为他工作的人。Lǎobǎn shì gùyōng tārén wèi tā gōngzuò de rén.

A baby is someone **whose** mother cares for him or her.

婴儿是（需要）母亲照顾他/她的人。Yīng'ér shì (xūyào) mǔqīn zhàogù tā de rén.

How to talk about two separate issues within the same sentence:

The house we're living in belongs to our relatives.

我们住的房子是属于我们亲戚的。Wǒmen zhù de fángzi shì shǔyú wǒmen qīnqi de.

The people we're talking to are our neighbours.

正在和我们交谈的人是我们的邻居。Zhèngzài hé wǒmen jiāotán de rén shì wǒmen de línjū.

The place we're going to is our favourite holiday destination.

我们正要去的地方是我们最喜欢的度假圣地。

Wǒmen zhèng yào qù de dìfāng shì wǒmen zuì xǐhuān de dùjià shèngdì.

The people (that) we met were kind and friendly.

我们所遇见的人是善良和友好的。Wǒmen suǒ yùjiàn de rén shì shànliáng hé yǒuhǎo de.

The car (that) he drove was modern and fast.

他驾驶的那辆车是现代的和快速的。Tā jiàshǐ de nà liàng chē shì xiàndài de hé kuàisù de.

The hotel (that) we stayed in was luxurious and expensive.

我们住的酒店是豪华和昂贵的。Wǒmen zhù de jiǔdiàn shì háohuá hé ángguì de.

The food (that) we ate was both delicious and plentiful.

我们吃的食物既美味又丰富。Wǒmen chī de shíwù jì měiwèi yòu fēngfù.

The sights (that) we saw were breathtakingly beautiful.

我们看到的景点令人叹为观止。Wǒmen kàndào de jǐngdiǎn lìngrén tànwéi guānzhǐ.

It is normal to want to place two simple sentences together to make a complex one:

Feeling exhausted, I went to bed early.

感到很用完，我早点睡觉了。Gǎndào hěn yòngwán, wǒ zǎo diǎn shuìjiào le.

I went to bed early because I was feeling tired.

我早点睡觉了，因为我感到很用完。Wǒ zǎo diǎn shuìjiào le, yīnwèi wǒ gǎndào hěn yòngwán.

She hurt her arm lifting the suitcase.

她抬起行李箱，伤了她的胳膊。Tā táiqǐ xínglǐxiāng, shāng le tā de gēbó.

Lifting the suitcase, she hurt her arm.

抬起行李箱，她伤了她的胳膊。Táiqǐ xínglǐxiāng, tā shāng le tā de gēbó.

The boys became thirsty playing football.

踢足球让男孩子们变得很口渴。Tī zúqiú ràng nán háizimen biànde hěn kǒukě.

Playing football, the boys became thirsty.

（因为）踢足球，男孩子们变得很口渴。(Yīnwèi) tī zúqiú, nán háizimen biànde hěn kǒukě.

He could play basketball well because he was tall.

他篮球能打得很好，因为他很高。Tā lánqiú néng dǎ de hěn hǎo, yīnwèi tā hěn gāo.

Being tall, he was able to play basketball well.

（因为）他很高，他篮球能打得很好。(Yīnwèi) tā hěn gāo, tā lánqiú néng dǎ de hěn hǎo.

Being talented at maths, he managed to calculate it.

因为在数学方面有天赋，他设法进行了计算。

Yīnwèi zài shùxué fāngmiàn yǒu tiānfù, tā shèfǎ jìnxíng le jìsuàn.

Simon managed to calculate it because he was talented at maths.

西蒙设法进行了计算，因为他在数学方面有天赋。

Xīméng shèfǎ jìnxíng le jìsuàn, yīnwèi tā zài shùxué fāngmiàn yǒu tiānfù.

Not being interested in it, she didn't understand how to do it.

因为对此不感兴趣，她当时不理解要怎么做。

Yīnwèi duìcǐ bù gǎn xìngqù, tā dāngshí bù lǐjiě yào zěnme zuò.

He didn't like to go out every night because he was often tired after work.

他当时不喜欢每天晚上外出，因为他下班后经常感到疲倦。

Tā dāngshí bù xǐhuān měi tiān wǎnshàng wàichū, yīnwèi tā xiàbān hòu jīngcháng gǎndào píjuàn.

Being/Feeling tired after work, he didn't like to go out every night.

因为工作后感到疲倦，他当时不喜欢每天晚上外出。

Yīnwèi gōngzuò hòu gǎndào píjuàn, tā dāngshí bù xǐhuān měi tiān wǎnshàng wàichū.

Paul didn't know how to start the car because he had never driven a car before.

保罗当时不知道怎么启动这辆车，因为他以前从没驾驶过汽车。

Bǎoluó dāngshí bù zhīdào zěnme qǐdòng zhè liàng chē, yīnwèi tā yǐqián cóng méi jiàshǐguò qìchē.

Never having driven a car before, Paul couldn't start it.

因为从来没有驾驶过汽车，保罗无法启动它。

Yīnwèi cónglái méi yǒu jiàshǐguò qìchē, Bǎoluó wúfǎ qǐdòng tā.

She didn't understand how to do it because she wasn't interested in it.

她当时不明白该怎么做，因为她对此不感兴趣。(对此 means 'in this regard')

Tā dāngshí bù míngbái gāi zěnme zuò, yīnwèi tā duì cǐ bù gǎn xìngqù.

She is **my** friend.

She is a friend of **mine**.

她是我的朋友。

Tā shì wǒ de péngyǒu.

They are **our** pets.

They are pets of **ours**.

它们是我们的宠物。

Tāmen shì wǒmen de chǒngwù.

This is **his** desk.

This is a desk of **his**.

这是他的桌子。

Zhè shì tā de zhuōzi.

Those are **her** Chinese books.

Those are Chinese books of **hers**.

那些是她的中文书。

Nàxiē shì tā de Zhōngwén shū.

Rodger's idea was very good.

罗杰的想法非常好。

Luōjié de xiǎngfǎ fēicháng hǎo.

That was **a very good idea of Rodger's**.

那是罗杰的非常好的主意。

Nà shì Luōjié de fēicháng hǎo de zhǔyì.

This pen **belongs to** me.

这支钢笔属于我。Zhè zhī gāngbǐ shǔyú wǒ.

This is **my own** pen.

这是我自己的钢笔。Zhè shì wǒ zìjǐ de gāngbǐ.

That bungalow belongs to my friend's uncle.

那栋平房属于我朋友的叔叔。 Nà dòng píngfáng shǔyú wǒ péngyǒu de shūshu.

That is my friend's uncle's **own bungalow**.

这是我朋友叔叔自己的平房。Zhè shì wǒ péngyǒu shūshu zìjǐ de píngfáng.

I never cut my hair.

我从不剪头发。 Wǒ cóngbù jiǎn tóufǎ.

I never cut **my own** hair.

我从不剪自己的头发。Wǒ cóngbù jiǎn zìjǐ de tóufǎ.

My father spends lots of time growing vegetables.

我父亲花很多时间种植蔬菜。Wǒ fùqīn huā hěn duō shíjiān zhòngzhí shūcài.

My father spends lots of time growing **his own** vegetables.

我父亲花很多时间种植自己的蔬菜。Wǒ fùqīn huā hěn duō shíjiān zhòngzhí zìjǐ de shūcài.

The use of 'all' in Mandarin (所有 + noun) and (所有的 + noun 都) is as follows:

All... (所有...都) For example, all animals in the world; all people on Earth.

例如：世界上所有的动物；地球上所有的人。

Lìrú: Shìjiè shàng suǒyǒu de dòngwù; dìqiú shàng suǒyǒu de rén.

All of the... (所有的...) For example, all of the children in the park; all of the food at the party.

例如：公园里所有的小孩；聚会上所有的食物。

Lìrú: Gōngyuán lǐ suǒyǒu de xiǎohái; jùhuì shàng suǒyǒu de shíwù.

All people think that environmental protection is essential.

所有人都认为环境保护是必要的。

Suǒyǒu rén dōu rènwéi huánjìng bǎohù shì bìyào de.

All animals and plants are important.

所有动物和植物都是重要的。

Suǒyǒu dòngwù hé zhíwù dōu shì zhòngyào de.

All countries in the world have their own unique features.

世界上所有国家都有自己独特的特征。

Shìjiè shàng suǒyǒu guójiā dōu yǒu zìjǐ dútè de tèzhēng.

All of the people at the party left rather late.

聚会上所有的人都离开得很晚。

Jùhuì shàng suǒyǒu de rén dōu líkāi de hěn wǎn.

All of the students in the class did well in the competition.

全班的学生都在比赛中表现得很好。

Quán bān de xuéshēng dōu zài bǐsài zhōng biǎoxiàn de hěn hǎo.

All of the dishes in this restaurant are too spicy.

那个饭馆里所有的菜都太辣了。

Nà gè fànguǎn lǐ suǒyǒu de cài dōu tài là le.

All of the/the whole family 全家 Quán jiā

All of the class/the whole class 全班级 Quán bānjí

The whole country/all of the country 全国 Quán guó

The whole/all of the month 全月 Quán yuè

All of my/Our whole family went to South America last year.

去年我们全家人都去了南美洲。

Qùnián wǒmen quán jiā rén dōu qù le Nán Měizhōu.

Some people don't like eating seafood.

一些人不喜欢吃海鲜。 Yīxiē rén bù xǐhuān chī hǎixiān.

Some of the people here don't like eating meat.

这里的**一些人**不喜欢吃肉。 Zhèlǐ de yīxiē rén bù xǐhuān chī ròu.

Most cars have many safety features these days.

如今，**大多数**汽车都有许多安全功能。

Rújīn, dà duōshù qìchē dōu yǒu xǔduō ānquán gōngnéng.

Most of the cars in this car park are quite expensive.

这个停车场的**大多数**汽车都很贵。

Zhè gè tíngchē chǎng de dà duōshù qìchē dōu hěn guì.

No people in this world know if aliens are real.

这个世界上**没有人**知道外星人是否真实。

Zhè gè shìjiè shàng méi yǒu rén zhīdào wàixīngrén shìfǒu zhēnshí.

None of the students in my class know if our school is closing down.

我班上的**学生都不**知道我们学校是否（正在）关闭。

Wǒ bān shàng de xuéshēng dōu bù zhīdào wǒmen xuéxiào shìfǒu (zhèngzài) guānbì.

None of them could understand what the teacher said.

都不他们能理解老师说了什么。

Dōu bù tāmen néng lǐjiě lǎoshī shuō le shénme.

Unit 92

他可能已经生病了，因为他没在工作。

那个星期他们可能没在家。

Unit 93

医生是帮助病人变好（恢复健康）的人。

主题公园是人们可以玩乐的地方。

Unit 94

正在和我们交谈的人是我们的邻居。

我们看到的景点令人叹为观止。

Unit 95

感觉很用完，我早点睡觉了。

因为在数学方面有天赋，他设法进行了计算。

Unit 96

她是我的朋友。罗杰的想法非常好。

我从不剪自己的头发。

Unit 97

所有动物和植物都是重要的。聚会上所有的人都离开得很晚。

去年我们全家人都去了南美洲。

Unit 98

一些人不喜欢吃海鲜。如今，大多数汽车都有许多安全功能。

我班上的学生都不知道我们学校是否（正在）关闭。

There are **few people** in the world who appreciate my artwork.

世界上**很少有人**欣赏我的艺术作品。Shìjiè shàng hěn shǎo yǒu rén xīnshǎng wǒ de yìshù zuòpǐn.

Few people really want to die young.

很少有人真的想英年早逝。Hěn shǎo yǒu rén zhēn de xiǎng yīngnián zǎoshì.

Few of the people at the party didn't enjoy themselves.

聚会里的人**很少**觉得自己过得不快乐。Jùhuì lǐ de rén hěn shǎo juéde zìjǐ guò de bú kuàilè.

Few of the books sold at the bookfair.

很少有书在书展会出售。Hěn shǎo yǒu shū zài shūzhǎn shàng chūshòu.

Little is known about Sara's death.

关于萨拉的死**很少**有人知道。Guānyú Sàlā de sǐ hěn shǎo yǒu rén zhīdào.

Little information exists regarding exactly how man evolved from the same ancestor as the chimpanzee. 关于人类如何从与黑猩猩相同的祖先进化而来的信息确切**很少**。Guānyú rénlèi rúhé cóng yǔ hēixīngxīng xiāngtóng de zǔxiān jìnhuà érlái de xìnxī quèqiè hěnshǎo.

Little of what is known about Sara's life is interesting.

萨拉的生活很有趣，这个是鲜为人知的。

Sàlā de shēnghuó hěn yǒuqù, zhè gè shì xiǎn wèi rénzhī de.

Little of what he said was understood by anyone.

他说的话**很少**被人理解。Tā shuō de huà hěn shǎo bèi rén lǐjiě.

Neither person knew the answer.

两个人都不知道答案。Liǎng gè rén dōu bù zhīdào dá'àn.

Neither of the people knew the answer.

两个人都不知道答案。Liǎng gè rén dōu bù zhīdào dá'àn.

Neither restaurant was open.

两家餐厅**都**没有开。Liǎng jiā cāntīng dōu méi yǒu kāi.

Neither of the restaurants was open.

两家餐厅**都**没有开。Liǎng jiā cāntīng dōu méi yǒu kāi.

We didn't visit **either art gallery**.

我们没有参观**任何**一个艺术画廊。

Wǒmen méi yǒu cānguān rènhé yī gè yìshù huàláng.

They had the choice to stay at **either hotel**.

他们可以选择入住这两家酒店的**任何**一家。

Tāmen kěyǐ xuǎnzé rùzhù zhè liǎng jiā jiǔdiàn de rènhé yī jiā.

We didn't visit **either of the art galleries**.

我们没有参观**任何**一个艺术画廊。

Wǒmen méi yǒu cānguān rènhé yī gè yìshù huàláng.

They had a choice of **either of the hotels**.

他们可以选择入住这两家酒店的**任何**一家。

Tāmen kěyǐ xuǎnzé rùzhù zhè liǎng jiā jiǔdiàn de rènhé yī jiā.

The adverbs 'quite' and 'pretty' both mean (相当), but 'rather' means (很):

This film is **quite** good.

这部电影**相当**不错。

Zhè bù diànyǐng xiāngdāng búcuò.

That view is **pretty** decent.

那个观点**相当**不错。

Nà gè guāndiǎn xiāngdāng búcuò.

These toys are **fairly** interesting to the children.

那些玩具对孩子**相当**有趣。

Nàxiē wánjù duì háizi xiāngdāng yǒuqù.

The weather is **rather** cold.

天气**很**冷。Tiānqì hěn lěng.

This soup is **rather** tasty.

这汤**很**好喝。

Zhè tāng hěn hǎo hē.

My best friend and I go out together **rather** a lot.

我最好的朋友跟我一起出去（的次数）**很**多。

Wǒ zuìhǎo de péngyǒu gēn wǒ yīqǐ chūqù (de cìshù) hěn duō.

When English speakers use 'quite' in the same way as 'completely' or 'extremely',
then (非常) and (完全) can be used:

This cocktail is **quite amazing**.

这种鸡尾酒**非常**棒。

Zhè zhǒng jīwěijiǔ fēicháng bàng.

I don't often agree with you, but on this I **quite agree** with you.

我一般不同意你的观点，但这次我**完全**同意你的观点。

Wǒ yībān bù tóngyì nǐ de guāndiǎn, dàn zhè cì wǒ wánquán tóngyì nǐ de guāndiǎn.

I 'can't quite + verb' (不太 + verb) and 'haven't quite + verb' (还没有 + verb):

The teacher talks too quickly. I **can't quite understand** what he is says.

老师说得太快了，我**不太明白**他在说什么。

Lǎoshī shuō de tài kuài le, wǒ bú tài míngbái tā zài shuō shénme.

They **haven't quite finished** their reports yet.

他们**还没有完成**他们的报告。

Tāmen hái méi yǒu wánchéng tāmen de bàogào.

The use of relative pronouns is essential, and here are examples of using relative pronouns (who, that, which) as subjects in Mandarin:

who:

The man **who** lives next door is a good friend of mine.

住在隔壁的男人是我的好朋友。Zhù zài gébì de nánrén shì wǒ de hǎo péngyǒu.

That woman **who** is living along the street is my cousin.

那个住在街上的女人是我的表姐。Nà gè zhù zài jiē shàng de nǚrén shì wǒ de biǎojiě.

A policeman is someone **who** catches criminals.

警察是抓捕罪犯的人。Jǐngchá shì zhuābǔ zuìfàn de rén.

that:

The food **that** is in the fridge is not for eating.

冰箱里的食物不能用于食用。Bīngxiāng lǐ de shíwù bù néng yòngyú shíyòng.

The child **that** always throws his ball into our garden is at the same school as my son's.

那个总是把球扔进我们花园的孩子和我儿子在同一所学校。

Nà gè zǒngshì bǎ qiú rēng jìn wǒmen huāyuán de háizi hé wǒ érzi zài tóngyī suǒ xuéxiào.

I work for a company **that** makes electrical appliances.

我在一家生产电器的公司工作。Wǒ zài yī jiā shēngchǎn diànqì de gōngsī gōngzuò.

which:

The map **which** was on my desk was very useful.

以前，我书桌上的地图非常有用。Yǐqián, wǒ shūzhuō shàng de dìtú fēicháng yǒuyòng.

The road **which** is near mine is very wide.

靠近我的路很宽。Kàojìn wǒ de lù hěn kuān.

She prefers stories **which** make her feel excited.

她更喜欢让她感到兴奋的故事。Tā gèng xǐhuān ràng tā gǎndào xīngfèn de gùshì.

who:

The man **who I see** living next door to me is a friend of mine.

住在我隔壁的那个男人是我的好朋友。

Zhù zài wǒ gébì de nà gè nánrén shì wǒ de péngyǒu.

That woman **who I know** is living along the street is my cousin.

那个我认识的住在这条街上的女人是我的表姐/妹。

Nà gè wǒ rènshi de zhù zài zhè tiáo jiē shàng de nǚrén shì wǒ de biǎojiě/mèi.

A policeman **who/whom I know** catches criminals.

一个我认识的警察抓住罪犯了。

Yī gè wǒ rènshì de jǐngchá zhuāzhù zuìfàn le.

that:

The food in the fridge **that I bought** this morning is not for eating.

我今天早上买的放在冰箱里的食物不是用来吃的。

Wǒ jīntiān zǎoshàng mǎi de fàng zài bīngxiāng lǐ de shíwù bú shì yònglái chī de.

I work for a company **that I know** makes electrical appliances.

我在一家我知道是制造电器的公司上班。

Wǒ zài yī jiā wǒ zhīdào shì zhìzào diànqì de gōngsī shàngbān.

The child **that I know** always throws his ball into our garden goes to the same school as my son's.

那个我认识的经常把球扔进我们花园的孩子，跟我儿子在同一所学校上学。Nà gè wǒ rènshì de

jīngcháng bǎ qiú rēng jìn wǒmen huāyuán de háizi, gēn wǒ érzi zài tóngyī suǒ xuéxiào shàngxué.

which:

The map on my desk **which** I borrowed from you was very useful.

那张放在桌子上的我从你那里借来的地图很有用。

Nà zhāng fàng zài zhuōzi shàng de wǒ cóng nǐ nàlǐ jièlái de dìtú hěn yǒuyòng.

The road **which** is near mine is very wide.

那条靠近我的路很宽。

Nà tiáo kàojìn wǒ de lù hěn kuān.

She prefers stories **which** I read to her which/that make her feel excited.

她更喜欢我给她读的能让她兴奋的故事。

Tā gèng xǐhuān wǒ gěi tā dú de néng ràng tā xīngfèn de gùshì.

whose:

A boss is a person **whose** employees work for him or her.

老板是雇佣员工为他或她工作的人。

Lǎobǎn shì gùyōng yuángōng wèi tā huò tā gōngzuò de rén.

I know a man **whose** mother is a soldier.

我认识一个男人，他的母亲是一名士兵。

Wǒ rènshi yī gè nánrén, tā de mǔqīn shì yī míng shìbīng.

I forgot the name of the person **whose** car I crashed.

我忘记了我撞车的那个人的名字。

Wǒ wàngjì le wǒ zhuàngchē de nà gè rén de míngzì.

whom:

Peter is the man **whom** I enjoy spending time with the most.

皮特是我最喜欢花时间跟他相处的人。

Pítè shì wǒ zuì xǐhuān huā shíjiān gēn tā xiāngchǔ de rén.

My father is the man **whom** I often argue with about politics.

我父亲是我经常争论政治的人。

Wǒ fùqīn shì wǒ jīngcháng zhēnglùn zhèngzhì de rén.

The people **whom** I work with are often helpful and patient.

我与之合作的人常常乐于助人，很有耐心。

Wǒ yǔ zhī hézuò de rén chángcháng lèyú zhùrén, hěn yǒu nàixīn.

where:

The place **where** I usually have my lunch is next to my company building.

我通常吃午餐的地方在我公司大楼旁边。

Wǒ tōngcháng chī wǔcān de dìfāng zài wǒ gōngsī dàlóu pángbiān.

The city **where** I spend most of my time is Rui'an.

我大部分时间都待在瑞安这座城市。

Wǒ dà bùfèn shíjiān dōu dài zài Ruì'ān zhè zuò chéngshì.

The place **where** I grew up has changed a lot in recent years.

我成长的地方近年来发生了很大变化。

Wǒ chéngzhǎng de dìfāng jìnnián lái fāshēng le hěn dà biànhuà.

Here are examples of using relative pronouns to add extra information:

My cousin, **who** often comes over for a quick chat, is my father's brother's daughter.

我的表姐/妹经常过来快速聊天，她是我父亲的兄弟的女儿。

Wǒ de biǎojiě/mèi jīngcháng guòlái kuàisù liáotiān, tā shì wǒ fùqīn de xiōngdì de nǚ'ér.

My best friend, **who** never goes out after 9:00 p.m., is usually very optimistic.

我最好的朋友通常都很乐观，他晚上九点后再也不出去了。

Wǒ zuìhǎo de péngyǒu tōngcháng dōu hěn lèguān, tā wǎnshàng jiǔ diǎn hòu zài yě bù chūqù le.

We stayed at an expensive hotel, **which** my uncle recommended to us.

我们住在一家昂贵的酒店，这是我叔叔向我们推荐的。(向 means 'to' such as 'apologise **to** us')

Wǒmen zhù zài yī jiā ángguì de jiǔdiàn, zhè shì wǒ shūshu xiàng wǒmen tuījiàn de.

My son's school, **where** he prefers to play basketball, is quite far from our house.

我儿子的学校，他更喜欢在那里打篮球，离我们家很远。

Wǒ érzi de xuéxiào, tā gèng xǐhuān zài nàlǐ dǎ lánqiú, lí wǒmen jiā hěn yuǎn.

Laura, **whose** mother is a great friend of my mother's, has invited us for lunch.

劳拉，她的母亲是我妈妈的好朋友，她邀请我们去吃午餐。

Láolā, tā de mǔqīn shì wǒ māma de hǎo péngyǒu, tā yāoqǐng wǒmen qù chī wǔcān.

Summary of units 99 – 105

Unit 99

很少有人真的想英年早逝。

关于萨拉的死很少有人知道。

Unit 100

两个人都不知道答案。

我们没有参观任何个艺术画廊。

Unit 101

这本电影相当不错。这种鸡尾酒非常棒。

我一般不同意你的观点，但这次我完全同意你的观点。

Unit 102

住在隔壁的男人是我的好朋友。冰箱里的食物不能用于食用。

靠近我的路很宽。

Unit 103

那个我认识的住在这条街上的女人是我的表姐/妹。 我在一家我知道是制造电器的公司上班。

那条靠近我的路很宽。

Unit 104

我认识一个男人，他的母亲是一名士兵。皮特是我最喜欢花时间跟他相处的人。

我成长的地方近年来发生了很大变化。

Unit 105

我们住在一家昂贵的酒店，这是我叔叔向我们推荐的。

劳拉，她的母亲是我妈妈的好朋友，她邀请我们去吃午餐。

If you are writing for a newspaper or simply reporting what someone told you, it is useful

to know how to report some facts or beliefs about someone or some situation:

It is said that the weather will be extremely hot tomorrow.

据说明天的天气非常得热。Jùshuō míngtiān de tiānqì fēicháng de rè.

It is alleged that the burglar had a few friends helping him.

据称窃贼有几个朋友帮他。Jùchēng qièzéi yǒu jǐ gè péngyǒu bāng tā.

It is believed that all the people survived the ferry sinking.

大家相信所有人都在渡轮沉没中幸存下来。

Dàjiā xiāngxìn suǒyǒu rén dōu zài dùlún chénmò zhōng xìngcún xiàlái.

She **is supposed to** be here by now.

她原本现在应该在这里。Tā yuánběn xiànzài yīnggāi zài zhèlǐ.

She **should be** here by now.

她现在应该在这里。Tā xiànzài yīnggāi zài zhèlǐ.

That film **was supposed to** be brilliant.

那部电影本来应该很精彩的。Nà bù diànyǐng běnlái yīnggāi hěn jīngcǎi de. (本来...的 for past)

That film **should have been** brilliant.

那部电影应该很精彩。Nà bù diànyǐng yīnggāi hěn jīngcǎi.

Please get dressed quickly. We're **supposed to** get there by 5:00 p.m.

请快点穿好衣服。我们应该在下午五点到达那里。

Qǐng kuài diǎn chuānhǎo yīfú. Wǒmen yīnggāi zài xiàwǔ wǔ diǎn dàodá nàlǐ.

We **should get** there by 5:00 p.m.

等到下午五点，我们应该到达那里。Děngdào xiàwǔ wǔ diǎn, wǒmen yīnggāi dàodá nàlǐ.

The man **is said to be** about 55 years old.

据说这名男人大约55岁。Jùshuō zhè míng nánrén dàyuē 55 suì.

It is said that he is about 55 years old.

据说他大约55岁。Jùshuō tā dàyuē 55 suì.

The criminal **is understood to be** known to the police.

据了解，警方对罪犯有所了解。Jù liǎojiě, jǐngfāng duì zuìfàn yǒu suǒ liǎojiě.

It is understood that the criminal is known to the police.

据了解，该罪犯是警方所知的。Jù liǎojiě, gāi zuìfàn shì jǐngfāng suǒzhī de.

He **is reported to have been caught** outside the shop.

据报道，他被抓到商店门外。Jù bàodào, tā bèi zhuādào shāngdiàn mén wài.

It is reported that he was caught outside the shop.

据报道，他被抓到商店门外。Jù bàodào tā bèi zhuādào shāngdiàn mén wài.

There is expected to be a royal ceremony for the President next week.

预计下周将要为总统举行皇家仪式。Yùjì xià zhōu jiāng yào wèi Zǒngtǒng jǔxíng huángjiā yíshì.

It is expected that there will be a royal ceremony for the President next week.

预计下周有一场皇家仪式要为总统举行。

Yùjì xià zhōu yǒu yī chǎng huángjiā yíshì yào wèi Zǒngtǒng jǔxíng.

The dog is believed to be running around the park without its owner.

据人们认为，狗在没有主人的情况下在公园里跑来跑去。

Jù rénmen rènwéi, gǒu zài méi yǒu zhǔrén de qíngkuàng xià zài gōngyuán lǐ pǎolái pǎoqù.

It is believed that the dog is running around the park without its owner.

据人们认为，狗在没有主人的情况下在公园周围跑来跑去。

Jù rénmen rènwéi, gǒu zài méi yǒu zhǔrén de qíngkuàng xià zài gōngyuán zhōuwéi pǎolái pǎoqù.

Here are examples of how to report information in Mandarin:

'I **want to** go to the nearest coffee bar for coffee.'

"我想去最近的咖啡吧喝咖啡。" "Wǒ xiǎng qù zuìjìn de kāfēiba hē kāfēi."

What did she say? 她说了什么？ Tā shuō le shénme?

She said that she **wanted** to go to the nearest coffee bar for coffee.

她说了她想去最近的咖啡吧喝咖啡。Tā shuō le tā xiǎng qù zuìjìn de kāfēiba hē kāfēi.

'I **can't** find anywhere to park my car.'

"我找不到任何地方停我的车。" "Wǒ zhǎo bú dào rènhé dìfāng tíng wǒ de chē."

What did he say? 他说了什么？ Tā shuō le shénme?

He said that he **couldn't** find anywhere to park his car.

他说了他找不到任何地方停他的车。Tā shuō le tā zhǎo bú dào rènhé dìfāng tíng tā de chē.

'I **won't** be living abroad in the future.'

"我在将来不会生活在国外。" "Wǒ zài jiānglái bú huì shēnghuó zài guówài."

"What did Laura say? 劳拉说了什么？ Láolā shuō le shénme?

She said that she **wouldn't** be living abroad in the future.

她说了她在将来不会生活在国外。Tā shuō le tā zài jiānglái bú huì shēnghuó zài guówài.

'I only **have** £500 in my bank account.'

"我银行账户里只有500英镑。" "Wǒ yínháng zhànghù lǐ zhǐ yǒu 500 yīngbàng."

What did he say? 他说了什么？ Tā shuō le shénme?

He said that he only **had** £500 in his bank account.

他说了他银行账户里只有500英镑。Tā shuō le tā yínháng zhànghù lǐ zhǐ yǒu 500 yīngbàng.

'I **am not happy** with my current career.'

"我对我现在是职业不满意。" "Wǒ duì wǒ xiànzài shì zhíyè bù mǎnyì."

What did he tell you?

他告诉了你什么？ Tā gàosù le nǐ shénme?

He told me **that he wasn't happy** with his current career.

他告诉了我他对自己现在的职业不是很满意。

Tā gàosù le wǒ tā duì zìjǐ xiànzài de zhíyè bú shì hěn mǎnyì.

'I **cannot spend time** with such an annoying person.'

"我不能把时间花在这样一个讨厌的人身上。"

"Wǒ bù néng bǎ shíjiān huā zài zhèyàng yī gè tǎoyàn de rén shēn shàng."

What did she tell you? 她告诉了你什么？ Tā gàosù le nǐ shénme?

She told me **that she couldn't spend time** with such an annoying person.

她告诉了我她不能把时间花在这样一个讨厌的人身上。

Tā gàosù le wǒ tā bù néng bǎ shíjiān huā zài zhèyàng yī gè tǎoyàn de rén shēn shàng.

'**Could you help** me choose the best colour?'

"你能帮我选一个最好的颜色吗？" "Nǐ néng bāng wǒ xuǎn yī gè zuìhǎo de yánsè ma?"

What did she ask you? 她问了你什么？ Tā wèn le nǐ shénme?

She asked me **if/whether I could help** her choose the best colour.

她问了我是否可以帮她选一个最好看的颜色。

Tā wèn le wǒ shìfǒu kěyǐ bāng tā xuǎn yī gè zuì hǎokàn de yánsè.

'**May I open** the window to let in some fresh air?'

"我能把窗户打开让新鲜空气流进来吗？"

Wǒ néng bǎ chuānghù dǎkāi ràng xīnxiān kōngqì liú jìnlái ma?

What did he ask you? 他问了你什么？ Tā wèn le nǐ shénme?

He asked me **if/whether I could open** the window to let in some fresh air.

他问了我是否可以把窗户打开让新鲜空气流进来。

Tā wèn le wǒ shìfǒu kěyǐ bǎ chuānghù dǎkāi ràng xīnxiān kōngqì liú jìnlái.

'looks as if/though' (看起来好像):

The man **looks as if** he is very angry.

他**看起来好像**很生气。or 他好像很生气。(好像 means 'seems')

Tā kànqǐlái hǎoxiàng hěn shēngqì. or Tā hǎoxiàng hěn shēngqì.

The apartment **looks as if** it is extremely expensive.

这座公寓**看起来好像**非常贵。

Zhè zuò gōngyù kànqǐlái hǎoxiàng fēicháng guì.

Our neighbours **sound as if** they are having a great party.

我们的邻居**听起来好像**在开派对/聚会。

Wǒmen de línjū tīngqǐlái hǎoxiàng zài kāi pàiduì/jùhuì.

This bed **feels as if** someone has already slept in it.

这张床**感觉好像**有人已经睡在里面了。

Zhè zhāng chuáng gǎnjué hǎoxiàng yǒurén yǐjīng shuì zài lǐmiàn le.

It **looks as though** the taxi is going to be late.

看起来租出车好像要晚点了。

Kànqǐlái zūchūchē hǎoxiàng yào wǎndiǎn le.

It **looks as though** there has been a car accident.

看起来好像发生了车祸。

Kànqǐlái hǎoxiàng fāshēng le chēhuò.

After what he said, it **sounds as though** he doesn't want to study at university.

在他说了这些以后，**听起来好像**他不想上大学。

Zài tā shuō le zhèxiē yǐhòu, tīngqǐlái hǎoxiàng tā bù xiǎng shàng dàxué.

She **drinks as if/though** it is the last drink in the world.

她**喝起来好像**这是世界上最后的饮料。

Tā hēqǐlái hǎoxiàng zhè shì shìjiè shàng zuìhòu de yǐnliào.

That dog eats **as if/as though** it hasn't eaten in a long time.

那只狗**吃起来好像**好久没吃东西了一样。

Nà zhǐ gǒu chīqǐlái hǎoxiàng hǎojiǔ méi chī dōngxī le yīyàng.

They **played** badminton **as if/though** they didn't care about winning.

他们**打起来好像**羽毛球他们不在乎赢。

Tāmen dǎqǐlái hǎoxiàng yǔmáoqiú tāmen bú zài hū yíng.

It seems that... (看来):

It seems that you have no interest in Chinese.

看来你对汉语没有感兴趣。

Kànlái nǐ duì Hànyǔ méi yǒu gǎn xìngqù.

It seems that they all enjoy going outside to play.

看来他们都更喜欢在外面玩。

Kànlái tāmen dōu gèng xǐhuān zài wàimiàn wán.

...makes you look... (显得):

Drinking like that **makes you look** uncivilised.

这样喝**显得**你不文明。

Zhè yàng hē xiǎndé nǐ bù wénmíng.

Speaking like that **makes you look** aggressive.

这样说话**显得**你很暴力。

Zhè yàng shuōhuà xiǎndé nǐ hěn bàolì.

not being able to (不是…, 而是…):

It's not that I don't want to help him, **but** I don't have enough time.

不是我不要帮他，**而是**我没有足够时间。Bú shì wǒ bú yào bāng tā, érshì wǒ méi yǒu zúgòu shíjiān.

It's not that she wanted to drink too much, **but** her friends encouraged her to drink too much.

不是她想喝太多了，**而是**他的朋友鼓励她喝太多了。

Bú shì tā xiǎng hē tài duō le, érshì tā de péngyǒu gǔlì tā hē tài duō le.

It's not that we cannot move to a new house this year, but I haven't found a new job yet.

不是今年我们不可以搬家，**而是**我还没找到新工作。

Bú shì jīnnián wǒmen bù kěyǐ bānjiā, érshì wǒ hái méi zhǎodào xīn gōngzuò.

Instead of... (不但不…, 反而…):

Instead of buying the groceries that I wanted, he bought meat and alcohol.

他**不但不**买我要的杂货品，**反而**买的肉和酒精。

Tā búdàn bú mǎi wǒ yào de záhuò pǐn, fǎnér mǎi de ròu hé jiǔjīng.

Instead of finishing work early, I had to stay late to finish extra work.

我**不但不**能早一点下班，**反而**不得不熬夜完成额外的工作。

Wǒ búdàn bù néng zǎo yī diǎn xiàbān, fǎnér bùdé bù áoyè wánchéng éwài de gōngzuò.

They left their tools in our house **instead of** taking them home with them.

他们**不但不**拿东西回家，**反而**把东西留在我的屋子里。

Tāmen búdàn bù ná dōngxī huíjiā, fǎnér bǎ dōngxī liú zài wǒ de wūzi lǐ.

The reason why... is because... (之所以..., 是因为...):

The reason why the shops are closed **is because** it's a public holiday today.

之所以今天商店都关门，**是因为**国定假日。

Zhī suǒyǐ jīntiān shāngdiàn dōu guānmén, shì yīnwèi guódìng jiàrì.

The reason why I am unable to do it **is because** I have never learned to do it.

之所以我做不到，**是因为**我从没有学会做。(The resultant complement 会 is used here, not 到)

Zhī suǒyǐ wǒ zuò bú dào, shì yīnwèi wǒ cóng méi yǒu xuéhuì zuò.

The reason why I was successful **was because** I worked 12 hours a day 7 days a week.

之所以我能成功，**是因为**我每天十二个小时工作。

Zhī suǒyǐ wǒ néng chénggōng, shì yīnwèi wǒ měi tiān shíèr gè xiǎoshí gōngzuò.

The reason why she didn't come **was because** she had a family matter with which to deal.

之所以她没来，**是因为**她有一个家庭事情要处理。

Zhī suǒyǐ tā méi lái, shì yīnwèi tā yǒu yī gè jiātíng shìqíng yào chǔlǐ.

The reason why they hadn't visited us before then **was because** they were always busy.

之所以他们还没有拜访我们，**是因为**他们一直很忙。

Zhī suǒyǐ tāmen hái méi yǒu bàifǎng wǒmen, shì yīnwèi tāmen yīzhí hěn máng.

Because I flew on business class, I felt relaxed when we landed.

我**因为**乘坐商务舱，**所以**降落的时候感到很放松。

Wǒ yīnwèi chéngzuò shāngwùcāng, suǒyǐ jiàngluò de shíhòu gǎndào hěn fàngsōng.

Unit 106

据说明天的天气非常得热。她原本现在应该在这里。

据报道，他被抓到商店门外。

Unit 107

"我找不到任何地方停我的车。他说了什么？

他说了他找不到任何地方停他的车。

Unit 108

"你能帮我选一个最好的颜色吗？"她问了你什么？

她问了我是否可以帮她选一个最好看的颜色。

Unit 109

这座公寓看起来好像非常贵。看起来租出车好像要晚点了。

她喝起来好像这是世界上最后的饮料。

Unit 110

看来他们都更喜欢在外面玩。

这样说话显得你很暴力。

Unit 111

不是今年我们不可以搬家，而是我还没找到新工作。

他不但不买我要的杂货品，反而买的肉和酒精。

Unit 112

之所以今天商店都关门，是因为国定假日。

她因为怀孕了，所以吃比较多。

It is useful to be able to say that you do not know something about a person or situation:

I don't understand **what** he said.

我不明白他**说了什么**。

Wǒ bù míngbái tā shuō le shénme.

I wasn't sure **how** to explain.

我不知道**怎么说明**（好）。

Wǒ bù zhīdào zěnme shuōmíng (hǎo).

I am not sure **which** shirts to buy.

我不确定买**哪**一件衬衫**好**。

Wǒ bú quèdìng mǎi nǎ yī jiàn chènshān hǎo.

None of us knew **who** she was.

我们都不知道她**是谁**。

Wǒmen dōu bù zhīdào tā shì shéi.

He doesn't know **where** he left his wallet.

他不知道把钱包留在**哪里了**。

Tā bù zhīdào bǎ qiánbāo liú zài nǎlǐ le.

Other useful phrases are 'I am afraid that...' (恐怕) and 'I thought that...' (以为):

I'm afraid that I am going to be late.

我**恐怕**要迟到了。Wǒ kǒngpà yào chídào le.

You haven't worked hard enough. **I'm afraid that** you cannot pass the test.

你还不够努力工作，我**恐怕**你不能通过考试。

Nǐ hái bú gòu nǔlì gōngzuò, wǒ kǒngpà nǐ bù néng tōngguò kǎoshì.

When I met her **I thought that** she was Japanese.

我见到她的时候，我**以为**她是日本人。Wǒ jiàndào tā de shíhòu, wǒ yǐwéi tā shì Rìběn rén.

We all **thought that** he was the boss.

在那时间，我们都**以为**他是老板。Zài nà shíjiān, wǒmen dōu yǐwéi tā shì lǎobǎn.

Unless (除非..., 否则...)

You cannot watch TV **unless** you have finished your homework.

除非你完成作业，否则你不可以看电视。

Chúfēi nǐ wánchéng zuòyè, fǒuzé nǐ bù kěyǐ kàn diànshì.

I will go out for a drink with friends tonight **unless** I have to work late.

除非我的工作到很晚，否则今晚我将和朋友出去吃晚饭。

Chúfēi wǒ de gōngzuò dào hěn wǎn, fǒuzé jīnwǎn wǒ jiāng hé péngyǒu chūqù chī wǎnfàn.

He wouldn't have done it **unless** somebody made him do it.

除非有人让他这样做，否则他不会这样做。

Chúfēi yǒu rén ràng tā zhè yàng zuò, fǒuzé tā bú huì zhè yàng zuò.

There was no way I was going to spend that much money **unless** it was fantastic.

除非它太棒了，否则我不会花那么多钱。

Chúfēi tā tài bàng le, fǒuzé wǒ bú huì huā nàme duō qián.

We can go out for dinner **unless** you'd prefer to cook something yourself.

我们可以出去吃饭，除非你自己愿意做饭。

Wǒmen kěyǐ chūqù chīfàn, chúfēi nǐ zìjǐ yuànyì zuòfàn.

I won't go out today **unless** it stops raining.

今天我不出去，除非雨停了。

Jīntiān wǒ bù chūqù, chúfēi yǔ tíng le. (了 indicates a possible change)

Unit 115:   as (while)... as (because of)...

as/when (的时候) or (当...时):

As I was walking along the beach, I saw children playing beach volleyball.

我沿着海滩散步**的时候**，我看到许多孩子在沙滩打排球。

Wǒ yánzhe hǎitān sànbù de shíhòu, wǒ kàndào xǔduō háizi zài shātān dǎ páiqiú.

I saw them talking to each other **as** I walked past them in the gym.

当我在健身房从他们身边走过**时**，我看到他们在交谈。

Dāng wǒ zài jiànshēnfáng cóng tāmen shēnbiān zǒuguò shí, wǒ kàndào tāmen zài jiāotán.

as/at the same time (一边..., 一边...):

She listened to music **as** she was cooking our dinner.

她**一边**做饭，她**一边**听音乐。Tā yībiān zuòfàn, tā yībiān tīng yīnyuè.

I usually eat dinner **as** I watch TV.

我**一边**看电视，**一边**经常吃晚饭。 Wǒ yībiān kàn diànshì, yībiān jīngcháng chī wǎnfàn.

as/because of (由于):

As it was raining hard, I decided to stay at home all day.

由于下雨得很大，我决定了整天呆在家里。

Yóu yú xiàyǔ de hěn dà, wǒ juédìng le zhěng tiān dāi zài jiā lǐ.

I left the birthday party early **as** I hadn't finished all my homework.

由于我还没有完成作业，我早早地离开了生日聚会。

Yóu yú wǒ hái méi yǒu wánchéng zuòyè, wǒ zǎozǎo de líkāi le shēngrì jùhuì.

As (two things happening over a long period of time):

As I spent years teaching Chinese, I learned to be patient and optimistic.

当我教了很多年汉语，我学会了耐心和乐观。

Dāng wǒ jiào le hěn duō nián Hànyǔ, wǒ xuéhuì le nàixīn hé lèguān.

Life in China became easier **as** I got used to living there.

随着我习惯了在中国生活，生活在中国变得更加放松。

Suízhe wǒ xíguàn le zài Zhōngguó shēnghuó, shēnghuó zài Zhōngguó biàndé gèngjiā fàngsōng.

Just as (就在..., 正...):

Just as the phone rang, I was getting up to go to the toilet.

就在电话响了的时候，我**正**起床上厕所。

Jiù zài diànhuà xiǎng le de shíhòu, wǒ zhèng qǐchuáng shàng cèsuǒ.

They were crossing the road **just as** I was walking out of the supermarket.

就在我走出了超市的时候，他们**正**过马路。

Jiù zài wǒ zǒuchū le chāoshì de shíhòu, tāmen zhèngguò mǎlù.

As soon as (一..., 就...):

As soon as I finish work, I go straight home and relax.

我**一**完成工作**就**直接回家放松一会儿。

Wǒ yī wánchéng gōngzuò jiù zhíjiē huíjiā fàngsōng yīhuìr.

My children started arguing together **as soon as** they woke up.

我的孩子**一**醒来**就**开始了争吵。

Wǒ de háizi yī xǐnglái jiù kāishǐ le zhēngchǎo.

once (一旦..., 就...):

Once I have made up my mind, I start doing it immediately.

我一旦确定的时候，我**就**马上开始做。

Wǒ yīdàn quèdìng de shíhòu, wǒ jiù mǎshàng kāishǐ zuò.

Once Laura felt comfortable in her new house, she decided to decorate it.

劳拉（**一旦**）在她的新房子感到舒服后，**就**确定了装饰。

Láolā (yīdàn) zài tā de xīn fángzi gǎndào shūfú hòu, jiù quèdìng le zhuāngshì.

In addition (此外), (还有), (另外) or (再说):

We have Chinese class tomorrow. **In addition**, you have 2 maths classes.

明天我们有中文课。**此外**，你有两节数学课。

Míngtiān wǒmen yǒu Zhòngwén kè. Cǐwài, nǐ yǒu liǎng jié shùxué kè.

Please remember that you have a test next week**. In addition**, you can use a dictionary.

请记住，下周你有考试。**还有**，你可以用字典。

Qǐng jìzhù, xià zhōu nǐ yǒu kǎoshì. Háiyǒu, nǐ kěyǐ yòng zìdiǎn.

I bought a new handbag, and **in addition** I bought some sunglasses.

我买了一个手包，**另外**买了一些太阳镜。

Wǒ mǎi le yī gè shǒubāo, lìngwài mǎi le yīxiē tàiyángjìng.

It is cold. Don't go out tonight! In addition, you don't have any warm clothes.

现在很冷。别今晚出去了。**再说**，你没有保暖的衣服。

Xiànzài hěn lěng. Bié jīnwǎn chūqù le. Zài shuō, nǐ méi yǒu bǎonuǎn de yīfú.

Moreover (并且) or (再说):

I think the story was entertaining. **Moreover**, it was not too long.

我觉得这个故事很有意思。**并且**，不太长。

Wǒ juéde zhè gè gùshì hěn yǒuyìsi. Bìngqiě, bú tài zhǎng.

I enjoy eating large amounts of meat. **Moreover**, it can make me stronger.

我享受吃很多肉。**再说**，吃肉让我变得更强大。

Wǒ xiǎngshòu chī hěn duō ròu. Zài shuō, chī ròu ràng wǒ biànde gèng qiáng dà.

not only..., but also (不但..., 而且...), (不但..., 不仅...) or (不仅..., 而且...):

That hotel is **not only** expensive **but also** too far from the city.

那家大酒店，**不但**很贵，**而且**离城市太远了。

Nà jiā dà jiǔdiàn, bú dàn hěn guì, érqiě lí chéngshì tài yuǎn le.

She is **not only** good at Chinese, **but also** good at speaking Japanese.

她**不但**擅长说中文，**而且**她还擅长说日本语。

Tā bú dàn shàncháng shuō Zhōngwén, érqiě tā hái shàncháng shuō Rìběn yǔ.

He is **not only** handsome, **but also** extremely clever.

他**不但**很英俊，**而且**非常聪明。Tā bú dàn hěn yīngjùn, érqiě fēicháng cōngmíng.

I can **not only** play poker well, **but also** many other card games.

我**不仅**打扑克比较好，**而且也**玩许多其他的纸牌游戏。

Wǒ bùjǐn dǎ pūkè bǐjiào hǎo, érqiě yě wán xǔduō qítā de zhǐpái yóuxì.

both... and... (又...又...) (This is used to show that a subject has two specific qualities):

These watches are **both** heavy **and** waterproof.

这些手表**又**重**又**防水。Zhèxiē shǒubiǎo yòu zhòng yòu fángshuǐ.

My father is **both** handsome **and** brave.

我父亲**又**英俊**又**勇敢。Wǒ fùqīn yòu yīngjùn yòu yǒnggǎn.

both...and... (既...又...) or (既..., 也...):

He can **both** run quickly **and** swim fast.

他**既**可以快速奔跑**又**快速游泳。Tā jì kěyǐ kuàisù bēnpǎo yòu kuàisù yóuyǒng.

She can **both** write beautiful poetry **and** sing elegant songs.

她**既**可以写出优美的诗歌，**也**可以唱优雅的歌曲。

Tā jì kěyǐ xiě chū yōuměi de shīgē, yě kěyǐ chàng yōuyǎ de gēqǔ.

Susan dislikes **both** impatient **and** lazy people.

苏珊**既**不喜欢没有耐心的人，**也**不喜欢懒惰的人。

Sūshān jì bù xǐhuān méi yǒu nàixīn de rén, yě bù xǐhuān lǎnduò de rén.

not only..., but even... (不但..., 甚至...):

Not only did I not go, **even** everybody else didn't go.

我**不但**没去，**甚至**其他人**都**没去。Wǒ bú dàn méi qù, shènzhì qítā rén dōu méi qù.

Not only did they buy a house, they **even** bought a new sports car.

他们**不但**买了一所房子哦，**甚至**他们也买了跑车。

Tāmen bú dàn mǎi le yī suǒ fángzi, shènzhì tāmen yě mǎi le pǎochē.

Not only are they extremely famous, they **even** live next door to our parents.

他们**不但**很有名，**甚至**他们住在我的父母隔壁。

Tāmen bú dàn hěn yǒumíng, shènzhì tāmen zhù zài wǒ de fùmǔ gébì.

Unit 113

我不明白他说了什么。他不知道把钱包留在哪儿了。

我恐怕要迟到了。

Unit 114

除非你完成了作业，否则你不可以看电视。

我们可以出去吃饭，除非你自己愿意做饭。

Unit 115

当我在健身房从他们身边走过时，我看到他们在交谈。我一边看电视，一边经常吃完饭。

由于我还没有完成作业，我早早地离开了生日聚会。

Unit 116

当我教了很多年汉语，我学会了耐心和乐观。就在电话响了的时候，我正起床上厕所。

我一完成工作就直接回家放松一下。

Unit 117

劳拉一旦在她的新房子感到舒服后，就确定装饰了。

Unit 118

我买了一个手包，另外买了一些太阳镜。

我觉得这个故事很有意思。并且，不太长。

Unit 119

不但…，而且…；不仅…，而且…；又 + adj 又 + adj；

既…，又…；既…，也…不但…，甚至连…

However (不过) or (然而):

Learning English is difficult; **however**, learning Chinese is more difficult.

学习英语比较难，**不过**学习中文更难。

Xuéxí Yīngyǔ bǐjiào nán, búguò xuéxí Zhōngwén gèng nán.

It is okay to exercise regularly, **however** not every day.

可以定期锻炼，**不过**不是每天锻炼。

Kěyǐ dìngqí duànliàn, búguò bú shì měi tiān duànliàn.

Although she didn't get the promotion, **nevertheless/however**, she did get a pay rise.

虽然她没有升职，**然而/但是**她获得加薪了。

Suīrán tā méi yǒu shēngzhí, ránér/dànshì tā huòdé jiāxīn le.

When I was young, I was bad at maths; **nevertheless/however**, when I grew up, I studied maths very well. 我小的时候，我不擅长数学，**然而/但是**我长大后，数学学得很好。

Wǒ xiǎo de shíhòu, wǒ bú shàncháng shùxué, ránér/dànshì wǒ zhǎng dà hòu, shùxué xué de hěn hǎo.

'however' (倒 + 也/又):

It is already late, b**ut/however** I don't feel tired.

已经晚了，我**倒也**不感觉很累。

Yǐjīng wǎn le, wǒ dào yě bù gǎnjué hěn lěi.

He works really hard, **however/but** his manager doesn't like him.

他很努力工作，他的经理**倒又**不喜欢他。

Tā hěn nǔlì gōngzuò, tā de jīnglǐ dào yòu bù xǐhuān tā.

You just graduated. You can celebrate **however** you like.

你刚才毕业了，你可以随意庆祝。

Nǐ gāngcái bìyè le, nǐ kěyǐ suíyì qìngzhù. or

你想怎么庆祝都可以。Nǐ xiǎng zěnme qìngzhù dōu kěyǐ.

Can I celebrate **however** I want?

我**怎么**庆祝**都**可以吗？Wǒ zěnme qìngzhù dōu kěyǐ ma?

Even though (Used when an activity is done frequently, or a fact is discussed)

Even if, (Used in theoretical situations)

Even when, (Used when an activity is done quite often)

Even though I am always busy with work, I still have time to go out with friends and play sports.

虽然我总是忙于工作，**但是**我有时间跟朋友一起出去运动。

Suīrán wǒ zǒngshì mángyú gōngzuò, dànshì wǒ yǒu shíjiān gēn péngyǒu yīqǐ chūqù yùndòng.

Even though she is my younger sister, we are **still** able to communicate well with each other.

虽然她是我妹妹，**可是**我们在一起交流得很好。

Suīrán tā shì wǒ mèimei, kěshì wǒmen zài yīqǐ jiāoliú de hěn hǎo.

Even though Linda didn't go to university, she **still** managed to get a great job.

即使琳达没去过大学上学，她**仍然**设法获得了极好的工作。

Jíshǐ Líndá méi qùguò dàxué shàngxué, tā réngrán shèfǎ huòdé le jíhǎo de gōngzuò.

Even if she cannot come, we can still go.

即使她不来，我们**也**可以去。

Jíshǐ tā bù lái, wǒmen yě kěyǐ qù.

Even if he doesn't have enough time, he is still going to enjoy himself.

即使他没有足够时间，他**也**会享受自己。

Jíshǐ tā méi yǒu zúgòu shíjiān, tā yě huì xiǎngshòu zìjǐ.

Even if you are very excited about sports, you still have to practise very hard.

即使你对运动感到兴奋，你**仍然**需要非常努力地练习。

Jíshǐ nǐ duì yùndòng gǎndào xīngfèn, nǐ réngrán xūyào fēicháng nǔlì de liànxí.

Even if I could afford it, I still don't want to buy it.

就是我买得起，我**也**不要买。Jiùshì wǒ mǎideqǐ, wǒ yě bú yào mǎi.

Even if they were married, they would still argue every day.

就是他们结婚了，他们**也**每天都争吵。Jiùshì tāmen jiéhūn le, tāmen yě měi tiān dōu zhēngchǎo.

Even if you hadn't said anything, I would have found out.

哪怕你没说话，我**也**会发现。Nǎpà nǐ méi shuōhuà, wǒ yě huì fāxiàn.

Even if he could take us there, he would say that he is too busy.

就算他能带我们去那里，他**也**会说他很忙。

Jiùsuàn tā néng dài wǒmen qù nàlǐ, tā yě huì shuō tā hěn máng.

Even when I was at home, I still never bothered to cook food myself.

即使当我在家里，**但是**我没有自己做饭。Jíshǐ dāng wǒ zài jiā lǐ, dànshì wǒ méi yǒu zìjǐ zuòfàn.

Even when she does cook dinner, she still takes too long.

即使当她做了晚饭，**但是**她花太多了时间。(做了 means 'does cook')

Jíshǐ dāng tā zuò le wǎnfàn, dànshì tā huā tài duō le shíjiān.

Even when he is in a good mood, he still doesn't help with the housework.

甚至在他的心情好的时候，他**也**不帮忙做家务。

Shènzhì zài tā de xīnqíng hǎo de shíhòu, tā yě bù bāngmáng zuò jiāwù.

Even when it was Christmas time, our relatives would still argue all day.

甚至在圣诞节期间，我们的亲戚**也**整天争吵了。

Shènzhì zài Shèngdànjié qījiān, wǒmen de qīnqi yě zhěng tiān zhēngchǎo le.

If you want to say 'even', there are two ways (甚至) or (连...都...):

Everyone enjoyed dinner, **even** the children did.

大家都享受晚饭了（尽情用餐），**甚至**孩子们**也**是。

Dàjiā dōu xiǎngshòu wǎnfàn le (jìnqíng yòngcān), shènzhì háizimen yě shì.

They like playing computer games, in the living-room, at school, **even** in the toilet.

他们都很喜欢玩电脑游戏，在客厅，在学校，**甚至**在卫生间**也**很喜欢。

Tāmen dōu hěn xǐhuān wán diànnǎo yóuxì, zài kètīng, zài xuéxiào, shènzhì zài wèishēngjiān yě hěn xǐhuān.

My father is too busy recently; he doesn't **even** have enough time to come home every day.

我爸爸最近太忙了，**甚至**他**也**没有足够的时间每天回家。

Wǒ bàba zuìjìn tài máng le, shènzhì tā yě méi yǒu zúgòu de shíjiān měi tiān huíjiā.

This story is simple to read, **even** young children can read it.

这个故事书很简单，**甚至**小孩子们**都**会看得懂。

Zhè gè gùshìshū hěn jiǎndān, shènzhì xiǎo háizimen dōu huì kàndedǒng.

This book is so easy that **even** my 10-year-old son understands it.

这本书很容易，**连**我十岁的儿子**都**看得懂。

Zhè běn shū hěn róngyì, lián wǒ shí suì de érzi dōu kàndedǒng.

This book is so difficult that **not even** my mother understands it.

这本书太难了，**连**我妈妈**都**看不懂。

Zhè běn shū tài nán le, lián wǒ māma dōu kànbudǒng.

To express 'don't/couldn't even' either (连...都...) or (一句...都...) is used:

She doesn't even trust her parents.

她**连**她父母**都**不相信。

Tā lián tā fùmǔ dōu bù xiāngxìn.

I can't even afford to buy a second-hand car.

我**连**二手汽车**都**买不起。

Wǒ lián èrshǒu qìchē dōu mǎibuqǐ.

You couldn't even help him.

你**连**他**都**没有不会帮。

Nǐ lián tā dōu méi yǒu bú huì bāng.

You didn't even have enough time to go out and play.

你**连**出去玩**都**没有足够时间。

Nǐ lián chūqù wán dōu méi yǒu zúgòu shíjiān.

I didn't even know where to buy a cup of coffee.

我**连**一杯咖啡**都**不知道哪里买。

Wǒ lián yī bēi kāfēi dōu bù zhīdào nǎlǐ mǎi.

She **didn't even** say anything about his accident.

她**一句**话**都**没说关于她的事故。

Tā yī jù huà dōu méi shuō guānyú tā de shìgù.

In some situations, you might wish to say that somebody is unable to do something that most people are probably able to do. It is not often used because it is slightly offensive, but you might wish to use it when talking to others about somebody else. For this either (更不用说) or (连..., 何况...) is used:

He can't (**even**) ride a bicycle, **let alone** drive a car.

他**都不**会骑自行车，**更不用说**开车。

Tā **dōu bú** huì qí zìxíngchē, **gèng bú yòng shuō** kāichē.

She doesn't (**even**) want to talk to me, **let alone** come to my house.

她**都不**要跟我说话，**更不用说**过来我的房子。

Tā **dōu bú** yào gēn wǒ shuōhuà, **gèng bú yòng shuō** guòlái wǒ de fángzi.

I can't (**even**) speak Chinese, **let alone** Japanese.

我**连**中文都不会说，**何况**会说日语。

Wǒ **lián** Zhòngwén dōu bú huì shuō, **hékuàng** huì shuō Rìyǔ.

I don't (**even**) have his phone number **let alone** know where he lives.

我**连**他的电话号码没有，**何况**知道他住在哪里。

Wǒ **lián** tā de diànhuà hàomǎ méi yǒu, **hékuàng** zhīdào tā zhù zài nǎlǐ.

I don't (**even**) play games at home, **let alone** play games at school.

我在家里**都不**玩游戏，**何况**是在学校。

Wǒ zài jiā lǐ **dōu bù** wán yóuxì, **hékuàng** shì zài xuéxiào.

If you want to talk about concessions, then 'although' (虽然/尽管…, 但是/可是…) is used:

Although she is very rich, (but) she is still not very happy with her life.

虽然她是一个富有的人，**但是**她还对她的生活不太高兴。

Suīrán tā shì yī gè fùyǒu de rén, dànshì tā hái duì tā de shēnghuó bú tài gāoxìng.

Although they enjoy playing sports at the weekend, (but) they seldom have spare time.

虽然他们在周末享受做运动，**可是**他们很少有空闲时间。

Suīrán tāmen zài zhōumò xiǎngshòu zuò yùndòng, kěshì tāmen hěn shǎo yǒu kòngxián shíjiān.

Although my sister is an adult, (but) she still hasn't travelled abroad yet.

我妹妹**虽然**是成年人，**可是**还没到国外去旅行。

Wǒ mèimei suīrán shì chéngnián rén, kěshì hái méi dào guówài qù lǚxíng.

(Although) she is very clever, (but) she still doesn't like to study hard.

虽然她很聪明，**可是**她不想努力学习。

Suīrán tā hěn cōngmíng, kěshì tā bù xiǎng nǔlì xuéxí.

Although she was often sad, (but) she used to go out with friends every weekend.

尽管她经常伤心，**可是**她曾经每个周末（都）跟朋友出去了。

Jǐnguǎn tā jīngcháng shāngxīn, kěshì tā céngjīng měi gè zhōumò (dōu) gēn péngyǒu chūqù le.

Although I was living in China for 5 years, (but) I never learnt to speak Chinese well.

尽管我在中国住了五年，**可是**我还是没有把中文说好。

Jǐnguǎn wǒ zài Zhōngguó zhù le wǔ nián, kěshì wǒ háishì méi yǒu bǎ Zhōngwén shuō hǎo.

Summary of units 120 – 126

Unit 120

…, however… (…, 不管…)；Although…, however… (虽然…, 然而/但是…)

…, however/but… (…, 倒 + verb)；however (随意 + verb)

Unit 121

虽然她是我的妹妹，可是我们在一起交流得很好。

即使他没有足够时间，他也会享受自己。　甚至在他的心情好的时候，他也不帮忙做家务。

Unit 122

就是他们结婚了，他们也每天都争吵。

甚至在他的心情好的时候，他也不帮忙做家务。

Unit 123

大家都享受晚饭了（尽情用餐），甚至孩子们也是。

在每个房间里有一台电视，连卫生间都有。

Unit 124

她连她父母都不相信。

她一句话都没说关于她的事故。

Unit 125

他都不会骑自行车，更不用说开车。

我在家里都不玩游戏，何况是在学校。

Unit 126

虽然她是富有的人，但是她还对她的生活不太高兴。

尽管我在中国住了五年，可是我还是没有把中文说好。

If you want to add information about the opposite kind of thing, then use 'otherwise' (要不然), (不然) or (否则):

Please hurry up, **otherwise** we will be late for the meeting.

请快一点走吧，**要不然**会议要迟到了。

Qǐng kuài yī diǎn zǒu ba, **yào bùrán** huìyì yào chídào le.

I couldn't find my notebook, **otherwise** I would know the answer.

我没找到笔记本，**要不然**我就知道答案了。(The 了 here indicates a theoretical change)

Wǒ méi zhǎodào bǐjìběn, **yào bùrán** wǒ jiù zhīdào dá'àn le.

She makes me go shopping with her, **otherwise** she won't help me with my homework.

她让我跟她一起去购物，**不然**她不帮我写我的作业。

Tā ràng wǒ gēn tā yīqǐ qù gòuwù, **bùrán** tā bù bāng wǒ xiě wǒ de zuòyè.

It is a good thing that I am not unhealthy, **otherwise** I could get sick easily.

幸运的是，我没有不健康，**不然**一定我很容易生病。

Xìngyùn de shì, wǒ méi yǒu bú jiànkāng, **bùrán** yīdìng wǒ hěn róngyì shēngbìng.

Fortunately, I brought an umbrella with me, **otherwise** we would have got wet.

很幸运，我带了一个雨伞，**否则**我们会被淋湿。

Hěn xìngyùn, wǒ dài le yī gè yǔsǎn, **fǒuzé** wǒmen huì bèi línshī.

You must study extra classes, **otherwise** you won't have a chance to pass the test.

你必须学习额外的课（补习班），**否则**你没有机会通过测试。

Nǐ bìxū xuéxí éwài de kè (bǔxí bān), **fǒuzé** nǐ méi yǒu jīhuì tōngguò cèshì.

In English the preposition 'by' is used extensively. So here are some examples of useful translations that might be necessary when speaking or writing Mandarin:

send a letter/parcel **by post**.

寄一封信/邮寄包裹。

Jì yī fēng xìn/yóujì bāoguǒ.

write a letter **by hand**.

用手写一封信。

Yòng shǒu xiě yī fēngxìn.

I contact you **by email/phone**.

我通过电子邮件/电话与你联系。

Wǒ tōngguò diànzǐ yóujiàn/diànhuà yǔ nǐ liánxì.

I always pay **by cash/credit**/debit **card**.

我总是用现金/用信用卡/转账卡支付。

Wǒ zǒngshì yòng xiànjīn/yòng xìnyòngkǎ/zhuǎnzhàng kǎ zhīfù.

I made a mistake **by accident**.

我偶然犯了一个错误。

Wǒ ǒurán fàn le yī gè cuòwù.

I met her **by chance** in the supermarket.

我在超市偶然遇见她了。

Wǒ zài chāoshì ǒurán yùjiàn tā le.

in the name of (以 + verb + noun + 的名义...):

I don't want to make this movie in my name.

不要**以**我**的名义**做这部电影。Bú yào yǐ wǒ de míngyì zuò zhè bù diànyǐng.

We should all buy fewer things in the name of reducing pollution.

以减少污染**的名义**，我们都必须买比较少的东西。

Yǐ jiǎnshǎo wūrǎn de míngyì, wǒmen dōu bìxū mǎi bǐjiào shǎo de dōngxī.

Another way to say 'when' is by using (等到..., 就/再...). Of course, 'by the time' also means 'when', so it can be expressed the usual way (...的时候) or (当...的时候); however, (到..., 就...) can be used:

By the time you finish this book, you will have (already) studied a lot of grammar.

等到你读完这本书，你就(已经)学了很多中文语法。

Děngdào nǐ dúwán zhè běn shū, nǐ jiù (yǐjīng) xué le hěn duō Zhōngwén yǔfǎ.

By the time the bus arrived, we had (already) waited for 45 minutes.

等公共汽车到达，我们就(已经)等了45分钟了。(了...了 to show it was longer than expected)

Děng gōnggòng qìchē dàodá, wǒmen jiù (yǐjīng) děng le 45 fēnzhōng le.

By the time/when the rain stops, I will go outside and look for a place to eat lunch.

等下雨停了，我再出去寻找吃中饭的地方。

Děng xiàyǔ tíng le, wǒ zài chūqù xúnzhǎo chī zhōngfàn de dìfāng.

When/By the time you get home, dinner will (already) be ready.

当你回家的时候，晚饭将准备好了。Dāng nǐ huíjiā de shíhòu, wǎnfàn jiāng zhǔnbèi hǎo le.

I was feeling exhausted **when/by the time** I got home.

我回家的时候，我感到很用完。Wǒ huíjiā de shíhòu, wǒ gǎndào hěn yòngwán.

When May arrives/**By** May this year, I will have been teaching Chinese for 6 years.

到今年五月，我就教了中文六年了。Dào jīnnián wǔyuè, wǒ jiù jiào le Zhōngwén liù nián le.

(了...了 to show that the person will continue teaching after May)

When December **comes**/**By** December, I will be 42 years old.

到十二月，我就42岁了。Dào shíèr yuè, wǒ jiù 42 suì le.

Here are examples of using (到) and (到那时) to express 'by' and 'by then/by that time', respectively.

by (到...):

I will finish this homework **by** Sunday evening.

到周日晚上，我**将**完成作业了。Dào zhōurì wǎnshàng, wǒ jiāng wánchéng zuòyè le.

I will have been married for 10 years **by** next year.

到明年，我**将**结婚了10年了。Dào míngnián, wǒ jiāng jiéhūn le 10 nián le.

She will have been working here for five months **by** October.

到10月，她**将**在这里工作了五个月了。Dào 10 yuè, tā jiāng zài zhèlǐ gōngzuò le wǔ gè yuè le.

by then/by that time (到那时):

I arrived at the cinema at 7:30, but **by then/by that time,** the movie had finished.

我七点半到达电影院，**但到那时**，电影已经结束了。

Wǒ qī diǎn bàn dàodá diànyǐngyuàn, dàn dào nà shí, diànyǐng yǐjīng jiéshù le.

If you come later, **by then/by that time**, we might have left.

如果你晚点来，**到那时**，我们有可能已经离开了。

Rúguǒ nǐ wǎn diǎn lái, dào nà shí, wǒmen yǒu kěnéng yǐjīng líkāi le.

For an activity continuing up to a certain point, either (直到) or (一直...到...) is used:

I will be working in Edinburgh **until** next Thursday.

直到下周四，我都在爱丁堡工作。Zhídào xià zhōusì, wǒ dōu zài Àidīngbǎo gōngzuò.

We will be at home **until** 12:00 p.m.

直到晚上12:00，我才在家里。Zhídào wǎnshàng 12:00, Wǒ cái zài jiā lǐ.

Father stayed at work **until** late into the evening.

爸爸**一直**工作**到**深夜。Bàba yīzhí gōngzuò dào shēnyè.

When expressing 'No matter what', (不管/无论..., 都...) is used:

No matter what she says, she still loves him.

不管她说了什么，她都一直爱着他。Bùguǎn tā shuō le shénme, tā dōu yīzhí ài zhe tā.

No matter what she does, she is always good at it.

不管她做什么，她都总是很擅长。Bùguǎn tā zuò shénme, tā dōu zǒngshì hěn shàncháng.

No matter when/whenever you come, I will be waiting for you.

不管你什么时候来，我都等你。Bùguǎn nǐ shénme shíhòu lái, wǒ dōu děng nǐ.

No matter what time it is, I will continue to work on the problem.

无论什么时候，我都会继续解决这道问题。

Wúlùn shénme shíhòu, wǒ dōu huì jìxù jiějué zhè dào wèntí.

No matter whose dirty washing it is, it must be put into the washing basket.

无论这是谁的脏衣服，都必须放入洗衣篮。

Wúlùn zhè shì shéi de zāng yīfú, dōu bìxū fàngrù xǐyīlán.

No matter which one you choose, you should choose carefully.

无论你选择哪一个，都必须谨慎选择。

Wúlùn nǐ xuǎnzé nǎ yī gè, dōu bìxū jǐnshèn xuǎnzé.

No matter where we go on holiday, at least we will be together.

无论你去哪里度假，至少我们会在一起。

Wúlùn nǐ qù nǎlǐ dùjià, zhìshǎo wǒmen huì zài yīqǐ.

No matter how you travelled around our city, you could always view its magnificent sights.

无论你去我们城市的哪个地方旅游，你随时可以欣赏到壮丽的风景。Wúlùn nǐ qù wǒmen

chéngshì de nǎ gè dìfāng lǚyóu, nǐ suíshí kěyǐ xīnshǎng dào zhuànglì de fēngjǐng.

No matter whether you change your career or not, you can always make money.

不管你是否改变自己的职业生涯，你总能赚钱。

Bùguǎn nǐ shìfǒu gǎibiàn zìjǐ de zhíyè shēngyá, nǐ zǒng néng zhuànqián.

'all' and 'every' and 'all' or 'every' (凡是..., 都...) can be used in the following way:

Whatever you say, I appreciate it.

凡是你说的，我总是都欣赏。

Fánshì nǐ shuō de, wǒ zǒngshì dōu xīnshǎng.

Everyone who has read this book will know it is great.

凡是看过这本书的人，都知道这很棒。

Fánshì kànguò zhè běn shū de rén, dōu zhīdào zhè hěn bàng.

Anyone who has helped me, will be remembered by me.

凡是帮忙过我的人，我都会记他们。

Fánshì bāngmáng guò wǒ de rén, wǒ dōu huì jì tāmen.

Anybody who is angry should not go out to a bar by themselves.

凡是生气的人，最好都不要一个人去酒吧。

Fánshì shēngqì de rén, zuìhǎo dōu bú yào yī gè rén qù jiǔbā.

Here are some other ways to say 'No matter what...' (怎么 + verb + 也):

No matter how I study, I can't remember it.

我怎么学也记不住。

Wǒ zěnme xué yě jìbuzhù.

No matter where I look, I still can't find it.

我怎么找也找不到。

Wǒ zěnme zhǎo yě zhǎobudào.

Another way to say 'No matter...' (不管..., 反正...):

No matter if she is embarrassed or not, she still needs to do the presentation.

不管她感觉不感觉尴尬，**反正**她还要做演讲。

Bùguǎn tā gǎnjué bù gǎnjué gāngà, fǎnzhèng tā hái yào zuò yǎnjiǎng.

No matter what you say, I am not interested.

不管你说什么，**反正**我没有兴趣。Bùguǎn nǐ shuō shénme, fǎnzhèng wǒ méi yǒu xìngqù.

No matter whether you want to study or not, you are going to study/must study.

不管你想学不学，**反正**你得去学。Bùguǎn nǐ xiǎng xué bù xué, fǎnzhèng nǐ deǐ qù xué.

No matter whether or not you understand, you will understand.

不管你懂不懂，你**反正**能懂。Bùguǎn nǐ dǒng bù dǒng, nǐ fǎnzhèng néngdǒng.

No matter how (就算再..., 也...):

No matter how clever she is, I still don't want to be her friend.

就算她**再**很聪明，我**也**不想成为她的朋友。

Jiùsuàn tā zài hěn cōngmíng, wǒ yě bù xiǎng chéngwéi tā de péngyǒu.

Not matter how much it costs, we should buy this house for our family.

就算再多的钱/**不管**多少钱，我们**也**应该为我们的家买这所房子。Jiùsuàn zài duō de qián/bùguǎn duōshǎo qián, wǒmen yě yīnggāi wèi wǒmen de jiā mǎi zhè suǒ fángzi.

You can change the form of 'No matter...' in the following way:

Whenever she arrives, we should be waiting for her.

不管她**什么时候**到达，我们都应该等她。

Bùguǎn tā shénme shíhòu dàodá, wǒmen dōu yīnggāi děng tā.

However it looks, they will be glad to receive it.

不管它看起来**怎么样**，他们会很高兴收到它。

Bùguǎn tā kànqǐlái zěnme yàng, tāmen huì hěn gāoxìng shōudào tā.

Whether you prefer meat **or** seafood, there is always a choice for everyone.

无论你更喜欢肉类**还是**海鲜，这是每个人的选择。

Wúlùn nǐ gèng xǐhuān ròu lèi háishì hǎixiān, zhè shì měi gè rén de xuǎnzé.

Whoever drinks the most alcohol is sure to be the silliest at the party.

无论**谁**喝最多的酒，肯定是聚会上最蠢的人。

Wúlùn shéi hē zuì duō de jiǔ, kěndìng shì jùhuì shàng zuì chǔn de rén.

Whomever you marry, I am sure you will be very happy.

不管你跟**谁**结婚，我相信你会很幸福（开心）。

Bùguǎn nǐ gēn shéi jiéhūn, wǒ xiāngxìn nǐ huì hěn xìngfú (kāixīn).

Whichever one is the best, they both still cost a lot of money.

无论**哪**一个是最好的，他们都花很多钱。

Wúlùn nǎ yī gè shì zuì hǎo de, tāmen dōu huā hěn duō qián.

Wherever you decide to study, you can always come back here at the weekends.

无论你决定**在哪里**学习，你都可以在周末回到这里。

Wúlùn nǐ juédìng zài nǎlǐ xuéxí, nǐ dōu kěyǐ zài zhōumò huídào zhèlǐ.

Whatever you do, you could still ask for help.

无论你**什么**做，你可以仍然请求帮忙。Wúlùn nǐ shénme zuò, nǐ kěyǐ réngrán qǐngqiú bāngmáng.

because (因为..., 所以...):

Because I don't have enough money, (**therefore**) I cannot buy any new things.

因为我没有足够钱，所以我不可能买新东西。

Yīnwèi wǒ méi yǒu zúgòu qián, suǒyǐ wǒ bù kěnéng mǎi xīn dōngxī.

Because she is an excellent student, (**therefore**) she is expected to get high scores in the test.

因为她是很好的学生，所以她被期望在考试中获得高分。

Yīnwèi tā shì hěn hǎo de xuéshēng, suǒyǐ tā bèi qīwàng zài kǎoshì zhōng huòdé gāofēn.

Because I have been busy recently, (**therefore**) I haven't had a chance to phone you.

因为我最近忙，所以没有机会给你打电话。

Yīnwèi zuìjìn máng, suǒyǐ méi yǒu jīhuì gěi nǐ dǎ diànhuà.

Because I haven't eaten anything today, (**therefore**) I am really hungry now.

因为我今天没吃东西，所以现在我好饿了。

Yīnwèi wǒ jīntiān méi chī dōngxī, suǒyǐ xiànzài wǒ hǎo è le.

Because I drank too much whiskey, (**therefore**) I had a bad hangover.

在那时，因为我喝太多了威士忌酒，所以我有宿醉严重。

Zài nà shí, yīnwèi wǒ hē tài duō le wēishìjì jiǔ, suǒyǐ wǒ yǒu sùzuì yánzhòng.

Because they had too much work to do, (**therefore**) they had no time to go out and have fun.

在那时，因为他们有太多了工作，所以他们没有时间出去外面玩儿。

Zài nà shí, yīnwèi tāmen yǒu tài duō le gōngzuò, suǒyǐ tāmen méi yǒu shíjiān chūqù le wàimiàn wánr.

because (..., 因此...):

I lived in Scotland for years, **therefore** I know how popular rugby is.

以前我在苏格兰住了很年，**因此**我知道橄榄球有多受欢迎。

Yǐqián wǒ zài Sūgélán zhù le hěn nián, Yīncǐ wǒ zhīdào gǎnlǎn qiú yǒu duōshòu huānyíng.

She is able to write quickly, **therefore** she finishes her homework very fast.

她能写很快，**因此**写完作业很快。

Tā néng xiě hěn kuài, yīncǐ xiěwán zuòyè hěn kuài.

Unit 127

请快一点走吧，要不然会议要迟到了。她让我跟她一起去购物，不然她不帮我写我的作业。

你必须学习额外的课（补习班），否则你没有机会通过测试。

Unit 128

我在超市偶然遇见了她。寄一封信/邮寄包裹。

不要以我的名义做这部电影。

Unit 129

等到你读完这本书，你就学了很多中文语法了。

当你回家的时候，晚饭将准备好了。

Unit 130

到周日晚上，我将完成作业了

如果你晚点来，到那时，我们有可能已经离开了。直到晚上12:00，我才在家里。

Unit 131

不管她说了什么，她一直爱着他。

无论你去哪里度假，至少我们会在一起。凡是看过这本书的人，都知道这很棒。

Unit 132

不管她什么时候到达，我们都应该等她。

无论你更喜欢肉类还是海鲜，这是每个人的选择。

Unit 133

因为我没有足够钱，所以我不可能买新东西。

以前我在苏格兰住了很年，因此我知道橄榄球有多受欢迎。

because of... (因为):

I didn't go out **because of** the rain.

我没有出门，因为这场雨。

Wǒ méi yǒu chūmén, yīnwèi zhè chǎng yǔ.

I never eat seafood **because of** the taste.

我从不吃海鲜，因为海鲜的味道。

Wǒ cóngbù chī hǎixiān, yīnwèi hǎixiān de wèidào.

Because of your parents, you can afford an apartment.

因为有的你父母，你可以买得起这所公寓。

Yīnwèi yǒu de nǐ fùmǔ, nǐ kěyǐ mǎideqǐ zhè suǒ gōngyù.

Because of my impatience, I made some mistakes at work.

因为我没有耐心，我在工作中犯了一些错误。

Yīnwèi wǒ méi yǒu nàixīn, wǒ zài gōngzuò zhōng fàn le yīxiē cuòwù.

The reason why... (的原因是):

The reason why some people don't study science is because of their lack of interest in it.

一些人没有学习科学**的原因是**他们缺乏兴趣。

Yīxiē rén méi yǒu xuéxí kēxué de yuányīn shì tāmen quēfá xìngqù.

The reason why they were late was because of the torrential rain.

他们迟到**的原因是**这场大暴雨。

Tāmen chídào de yuányīn shì zhè chǎng dà bàoyǔ.

Because we weren't able to buy the house, we couldn't move from our old one.

因为我们没有能力买房子，所有我们不能从老房子搬走。

Yīnwèi wǒmen méi yǒu nénglì mǎi fángzi, suǒyǒu wǒmen bù néng cóng lǎo fángzi bānzǒu.

Because everyone at the meeting had different opinions, no agreement was reached.

因为开会的每个人都有了不同的意见，没有达成任何协议。

Yīnwèi kāihuì de měi gè rén dōu yǒu le bùtóng de yìjiàn, méi yǒu dáchéng rènhé xiéyì.

Because it's hot today, it is okay if we go to the beach to sunbathe.

由于今天很热，我们可以去海边晒太阳。

Yóu yú jīntiān hěn rè, wǒmen kěyǐ qù hǎibiān shàitàiyáng.

Because you play basketball very well, it might be possible for you to go to some competitions.

由于你打篮球打得很好，就有可能参加一些比赛。

Yóu yú nǐ dǎ lánqiú dǎ de hěn hǎo, jiù yǒu kěnéng cānjiā yīxiē bǐsài.

As long as (只要... 就...) This is used for individual people or specific groups:

As long as you study hard, you will get a good score.

只要你努力学习，**就**会获得一个好的分数。

Zhǐyào nǐ nǔlì xuéxí, jiù huì huòdé yī gè hǎo de fēnshù.

As long as you finish your homework, then you can watch TV.

只要你完成作业，**就**可以看电视。

Zhǐyào nǐ wánchéng zuòyè, jiù kěyǐ kàn diànshì.

You must do as I say **as long as** you live here.

只要你住在这里，**就**必须照我说的做。

Zhǐyào nǐ zhù zài zhèlǐ, nǐ jiù bìxū zhào wǒ shuō de zuò.

There are many options available **as long as** you go to a good university.

只要你去一所好大学，你**就**有很多选择。

Zhǐyào nǐ qù yī suǒ hǎo dàxué, nǐ jiù yǒu hěn duō xuǎnzé.

As long as...' (凡是..., 都.../凡是..., 就...) This is used for 'the majority of people' in the world:

As long as you don't commit a crime, you can live freely.

凡是你不罪犯，**都**自由生活。Fánshì nǐ bú zuìfàn, dōu zìyóu shēnghuó.

As long as you obtain a visa, you can enter China.

凡是你获得签证，**就**可以进入中国。Fánshì nǐ huòdé qiānzhèng, jiù kěyǐ jìnrù Zhōngguó.

Providing that/if... (如果/只要):

Providing that it doesn't rain, the party should be fine.

只要没有下雨，派对就会很好。

Zhǐyào méi yǒu xiàyǔ, pàiduì jiù huì hěn hǎo.

Providing that there are no other issues, your computer should work fine now.

只要没有其他的问题，你的电脑就能正常工作。

Zhǐyào méi yǒu qítā de wèntí, nǐ de diànnǎo jiù néng zhèngcháng gōngzuò.

There won't be any problems, **providing that** we prepare everything carefully.

不会有任何问题，只要我们准备一切都很仔细。

Bú huì yǒu rènhé wèntí, zhǐyào wǒmen zhǔnbèi yīqiè dōu hěn zǐxì.

Provided that/if (假如):

Provided that Louis isn't late, everybody can start watching the film on time.

只要路易斯不迟到，大家可以准时看电影。

Zhǐyào Lùyìsī bù chídào, dàjiā kěyǐ zhǔnshí kàn diànyǐng.

There should be enough food and drink for everyone, **provided that** people aren't too greedy.

只要人们不太贪心，每个人都应该有足够的食物和饮料。

Zhǐyào rénmen bú tài tānxīn, měi gè rén dōu yīnggāi yǒu zúgòu de shíwù hé yǐnliào.

The trip should be educational, **provided that** all the students listen to the teacher carefully.

这个旅行应该是有教育意义的，**只要/前提是**学生都听老师听得小心。

Zhè gè lǚxíng yīnggāi shì yǒu jiàoyù yìyì de, zhǐyào/qiántí shì xuéshēng dōu tīng lǎoshī tīng de xiǎoxīn.

Do it the way... (试着像 + noun + 那样做吧):

I don't know how to fix this door. Well, try and **do it the way** your father does.

我不知道怎么修这扇门。 好吧，**试着像**你父亲**那样做吧**。

Wǒ bù zhīdào zěnme xiū zhè shànmén. Hǎo ba, shìzhe xiàng nǐ fùqīn nà yàng zuò ba.

Well, try and **do it as/like** your father does.

好吧，**试着像**你父亲**那样做吧**。Hǎo ba, shìzhe xiàng nǐ fùqīn nà yàng zuò ba.

Well, try and **do it as/like** your father showed you.

好吧，试着**像你**父亲给你做的**那样做吧**。

Hǎo ba, shìzhe xiàng nǐ fùqīn gěi nǐ zuò de nà yàng zuò ba.

I don't know how to do it. Just **do it as** your friend does.

我不知道怎么做，**就像**你朋友做的**那样做吧**。

Wǒ bù zhīdào zěnme zuò, jiù xiàng nǐ péngyǒu zuò de nà yàng zuò ba.

Just **do it like** your friend does.

像你朋友做的**那样做吧**。Xiàng nǐ péngyǒu zuò de nà yàng zuò ba.

Just **do it as/like** your friend showed you.

像你朋友给你看的**那样做吧**。Xiàng nǐ péngyǒu gěi nǐ kàn de nà yàng zuò ba.

this way (这样):

It is not too bad to study **like this**.

这样学，不太好。

Zhè yàng xué, bú tài hǎo.

It is not clear writing **like this**.

这样写，不清楚。

Zhè yàng xiě, bù qīngchǔ.

In regard to... (至于 + noun), (就 + noun) or (在 + noun 上):

I prefer Edinburgh. **With regard to** countries I prefer Austria.

我更喜欢爱丁堡。**至于**国家，就更喜欢奥德利。

Wǒ gèng xǐhuān Àidīngbǎo. Zhìyú guójiā, jiù gèng xǐhuān Àodélì.

In regard to when we have to leave, I am not yet certain.

至于什么时候离开，我还没确定。

Zhìyú shénme shíhòu líkāi, wǒ hái méi quèdìng.

As for/Regarding environmental pollution, the whole world needs to work together.

就环境污染，全世界都需要共同努力。

Jiù huánjìng wūrǎn, quán shìjiè dōu xūyào gòngtóng nǔlì.

In regard to company policy, you mustn't leave work before 5:00 p.m.

就公司政策，你不得在五点钟以前下班。

Jiù gōngsī zhèngcè, nǐ bùdé zài wǔ diǎn zhōng yǐqián xiàbān.

Regarding the city's economy, I think that it is quite robust.

在这座城市的经济上，我觉得它是相当粗放的。

Zài zhè zuò chéngshì de jīngjì shàng, wǒ juéde tā shì xiāngdāng cūfàng de.

In regard to your health issue, you need only go out and walk 5 days a week.

在你的健康问题上，你只需要每周出去走五次。

Zài nǐ de jiànkāng wèntí shàng, nǐ zhǐ xūyào měi zhōu chūqù zǒu wǔ cì.

As for (noun + 的话), As a result of (..., 结果...):

As for Shanghai, an abundance of foreign people come here every year.

上海**的话**，每年许许多多外国人来到。

Shànghǎi de huà, měi nián xǔxǔ duōduō wàiguó rén láidào.

As for you, I think you should meet a woman and get married.

至于你**的话**，我认为你应该找到一个美女，并且跟她在一起结婚。

Zhìyú nǐ de huà, wǒ rènwéi nǐ yīnggāi zhǎodào yī gè měinǚ, bìngqiě gēn tā zài yīqǐ jiéhūn.

As a result (结果):

He didn't revise, and **as a result**, he failed the test.

他没有复习，**结果**测试失败了。

Tā méi yǒu fùxí, jiéguǒ cèshì shībài le.

I was very afraid, and **as a result** I didn't play well.

我很害怕，**结果**玩/表现得不好了。

Wǒ hěn hàipà, jiéguǒ wán/biǎoxiàn de bù hǎo le.

any more/any longer (不再...了) or (不...了):

I don't play tennis **any longer/any more**.

我**不再**打网球了。 Wǒ bú zài dǎ wǎngqiú le.

He doesn't sell mobile phones **any longer/any more**.

他**不再**卖手机**了**。Tā bú zài mài shǒujī le.

I don't play tennis **now**. = He doesn't play tennis **any longer**.

我现在**不**打网球**了**。Wǒ xiànzài bù dǎ wǎngqiú le.

He doesn't sell mobile phones **now**. = He doesn't sell mobile phones **any longer**.

他现在**不**卖手机**了**。Tā xiànzài bú mài shǒujī le.

no longer (再也不), anyway (反正):

He **no longer** flies kites in the park.

他**再也不**去公园放风筝了。Tā zài yě bú qù gōngyuán fàng fēngzhēng le.

They can **no longer** stay in their jobs.

他们**再也不**能留在自己的工作上了。Tāmen zài yě bù néng liú zài zìjǐ de gōngzuò shàng le.

I'm not going out **anyway**.

反正我不出去。Fǎnzhèng wǒ bù chūqù.

Everyone in my family knows **anyway**.

反正家里的所有的人都知道了。Fǎnzhèng jiā lǐ de suǒyǒu de rén dōu zhīdào le.

Sometimes you might want to talk about doing something in the same way as it was done previously:

Do your homework **as/like I showed you** before.

按我以前给你看的**那样做**作业。

Àn wǒ yǐqián gěi nǐ kàn de nà yàng zuò zuoyè.

Make sure you leave everything **as/like it was** before you arrived.

确保这些东西跟你还没有来以前**一样**。

Quèbǎo zhèxiē dōngxī gēn nǐ hái méi yǒu lái yǐqián yīyàng.

Please be as honest **as** you **have always been**.

请你诚实**像**你**一直以来的样子**。

Qǐng nǐ chéngshí xiàng nǐ yīzhí yǐlái de yàngzi.

He **looks as I did** when I started my first day here.

当我开始我的第一天工作，他**看起来就像**是我做的一样。

Dāng wǒ kāishǐ wǒ de dì yī tiān gōngzuò, tā kànqǐlái jiù xiàng shì wǒ zuò de yīyàng.

as + pronoun + verb (正如我所):

You cannot do **as you wish** at school.

在学校你无法做到**正如你所愿**。

Zài xuéxiào nǐ wúfǎ zuòdào Zhèngrú nǐ suǒyuàn.

I am going to get that thing for you **as I promised**.

正如我所承诺的，我会给你拿那个东西。

Zhèngrú wǒ suǒ chéngnuò de, wǒ huì gěi nǐ ná nà gè dōngxī.

He did **as** I **expected**.

他做的**正如我所期望的那样**。

Tā zuò de **zhèngrú wǒ suǒ qīwàng de nà yàng**.

As a + noun (作为 + noun) or (当作 + noun):

As a teacher, I must encourage my students to do better.

作为一名老师，我必要鼓励我的学生做得更好。

Zuòwéi yī míng lǎoshī, wǒ bìyào gǔlì wǒ de xuéshēng zuò de gèng hǎo.

I worked **as a** taxi driver about 10 years ago.

十年以前我**做过**租出车司机。

Shí nián yǐqián wǒ **zuòguò** zūchūchē sījī.

I think of her **as a** friend.

我想起**把**她**当作**我的朋友。

Wǒ xiǎngqǐ **bǎ** tā **dàngzuò** wǒ de péngyǒu.

Summary of units 134 – 140

Unit 134

因为有的你父母，你可以买得起这所公寓。

一些人没有学习科学的原因是他们缺乏兴趣。由于今天很热，我们可以去海边晒太阳。

Unit 135

只要你努力学习，就会获得一个好的分数。

Unit 136

只要没有下雨，派对就会很好

这个旅行应该是有教育意义的，只要/前提是学生都听老师听得小心。

Unit 137

好吧，试着像你父亲那样做吧。

像你朋友做的那样做吧。

Unit 138

With regard to (至于 + noun) Regarding/as for (就...+ noun); (在 + noun 上, ...)

As for (noun + 的话, ...) As a result of (结果...了, ...)

Unit 139

我不再打网球了。我现在不打网球了。

他们再也不能留在自己的工作上了。反正我不出去。

Unit 140

当我开始我的第一天工作，他看起来就像是我做的一样。

他做的正如我所期望的那样。作为一名老师，我必要鼓励我的学生做得更好

In contrast (与此相反), Conversely (反过来):

She can swim quickly; **in contrast**, she runs very slowly.

她游泳很快，**与此相反**，她跑步很慢。

Tā yóuyǒng hěn kuài, yǔcǐ xiāngfǎn, tā pǎobù hěn màn.

He remembers numbers easily; **in contrast**, he forgets words easily.

他很容易记住数字，**与此相反**，生词忘记得很快。

Tā hěn róngyì jì zhù shùzì, yǔcǐ xiāngfǎn, shēngcí wàngjì de hěn kuài.

If you are a good son, you should always help your mother; **conversely**, if you don't help her then you are not a good son. 如果你是很好的儿子，你应该总是帮你妈妈。**反过来**，如果你不帮她，你是不好的儿子。Rúguǒ nǐ shì hěn hǎo de érzi, nǐ yīnggāi zǒngshì bāng nǐ māma. Fǎnguòlái, rúguǒ nǐ bù bāng tā, nǐ shì bù hǎo de érzi.

She agrees that it is necessary to focus on her original plan; **conversely**, she disagrees that no amendments can be made to it. 她同意专注于原计划很必要，**反过来**，她不同意不可能有修订。Tā tóngyì zhuānzhù yúyuán jìhuà hěn bìyào, fǎnguòlái, tā bù tóngyì bù kěnéng yǒu xiūdìng.

on the other hand (一方面… 另一方面…):

She will pass the exam. **On one hand** she is very clever; **on the other hand**, she is hardworking.

她会通过考试。**一方面**她很聪明，**另一方面**他很用功。

Tā huì tōngguò kǎoshì. Yī fāngmiàn tā hěn cōngmíng, lìng yī fāngmiàn tā hěn yònggōng.

When talking about a situation happening, even though something else could be stopping it from happening, 'despite' and 'in spite of' (尽管) are used:

Despite the rain, we (still) went out.

尽管下雨，我们还是出去了。Jǐnguǎn xiàyǔ, wǒmen háishì chūqù le.

Despite his hard work, he still couldn't pass the test.

尽管他努力学习，但是他仍然不能通过考试了。

Jǐnguǎn tā nǔlì xuéxí, dànshì tā réngrán bù néng tōngguò kǎoshì le.

In spite of being afraid of flying, I will fly to England next week.

尽管我害怕乘坐飞机，我下周还是会飞往英国。

Jǐnguǎn wǒ hàipà chéngzuò fēijī, wǒ xià zhōu háishì huì fēi wǎng Yīngguó.

In spite of the terrible traffic, we still go to work by car every day.

尽管交通跟糟糕，我们仍然每天开车去上班。

Jǐnguǎn jiāotōng gēn zāogāo, wǒmen réngrán měi tiān kāichē qù shàngbān.

If there are any exceptions that are in some way related to other subjects in the sentence, then you can use 'except' or 'besides' (除了):

Except you, who is good at sports in your family?

除了你以外，在你家庭谁擅长运动？

Chúle nǐ yǐwài, zài nǐ jiātíng shéi shàncháng yùndòng?

Besides our children, there are still many students here.

除了我们的孩子们，还有很多学生在这里。

Chúle wǒmen de háizimen, hái yǒu hěn duō xuéshēng zài zhèlǐ.

'in case' (以防), 'just in case' (以防万一) and 'in case of" (...的情况下):

In case she wants some fruit, I will go out and buy some.

以防她想要水果，我就出去买一些。Yǐfáng tā xiǎng yào shuǐguǒ, wǒ jiù chūqù mǎi yīxiē.

Take this warm coat **in case** it gets cold.

把这件暖和的外套拿去，**以防**天气变冷。

Bǎ zhè jiàn nuǎnhuo de wàitào náqù, yǐfáng tiānqì biàn lěng.

Could you write that down **in case** I forget, please?

以防我忘了，你能把它写下来吗？Yǐfáng wǒ wàng le, nǐ néng bǎ tā xiě xiàlái ma?

Take some extra money **just in case** you spend too much.

带一些额外的钱，**以防万一**你花太多了。Dài yīxiē éwài de qián, yǐfáng wànyī nǐ huā tài duō le.

Bring your reading glasses **just in case** you need to read something.

带上你的阅读眼镜，**以防万一**你需要读一些东西。

Dài shàng nǐ de yuèdú yǎnjìng, yǐfáng wànyī nǐ xūyào dú yīxiē dōngxī.

I always keep my mobile switched on **just in case** my girlfriend calls.

我总是保持我的手机打开，**以防万一**我的女朋友打电话给我。

Wǒ zǒngshì bǎochí wǒ de shǒujī dǎkāi, yǐfáng wànyī wǒ de nǚ péngyǒu dǎ diànhuà gěi wǒ.

In case of emergency, please take the stairs.

在紧急**的情况**下，请走楼梯。Zài jǐnjí de qíngkuàng xià, qǐng zǒu lóutī.

In case of fire, exit the building via the stairs.

在发生火灾**的情况下**，通过楼梯离开大楼。

Zài fāshēng huǒzāi de qíngkuàng xià, tōngguò lóutī líkāi dàlóu.

In case of any future problems, call this number.

在未来有任何问题（**的情况下**），打电话这个号码。

Zài wèilái yǒu rènhé wèntí (de qíngkuàng xià), dǎ diànhuà zhè gè hàomǎ.

There are 3 useful ways to say 'in order to' that are commonly used in Chinese:

I drove slowly **in order to** save petrol.

我慢慢地开车，**以便**省燃料。Wǒ mànman de kāichē, yǐbiàn shěng ránliào.

We worked more quickly **in order to** finish sooner.

我们工作得更快了，**以便**快点结束。Wǒmen gōngzuò de gèng kuài le, yǐbiàn kuài diǎn jiéshù.

I told him to help them **in order to** finish more quickly.

我告诉了他去帮助他们，**以便更快**结束。Wǒ gàosù le tā qù bāngzhù tāmen, yǐbiàn gèng kuài jiéshù.

I eat meat **in order to** become strong.

我总是吃牛肉，**好**变得强壮。Wǒ zǒngshì chī niúròu, hǎo biànde qiángzhuàng.

Mary exercised regularly **in order to** keep slim.

玛丽经常地锻炼，**好**保持苗条。Mǎlì jīngcháng de duànliàn, hǎo bǎochí miáotiáo.

My wife drinks green tea **in order to** stay healthy.

我的妻子喝绿茶，**好**保持健康。Wǒ de qīzi hē lǜchá, hǎo bǎochí jiànkāng.

In order to succeed, you need to go one step further.

为了成功，你必要就进一步。Wèi le chénggōng, nǐ bìyào jiù jìn yī bù.

She had to practise further maths **in order to** go to Beijing University.

为了她去北京大学上学，她就进一步学数学。

Wèi le tā qù Běijīng Dàxué shàngxué, tā jiù jìn yī bù xué shùxué.

You need to study further English **in order to/if you want to** study in America.

如果你**要**在美国学习的话，你就进一步学英语。

Rúguǒ nǐ yào zài Měiguó xuéxí de huà, nǐ jiù jìn yī bù xué Yīngyǔ.

Adjective + with:

I was **angry/annoyed about** his behaviour.

我对他的行为很**生气**。Wǒ duì tā de xíngwéi hěn shēngqì.

I was **angry/annoyed with** him.

我对他很**生气**。Wǒ duì tā hěn shēngqì.

Are you **satisfied with** your life so far?

到目前为止，你**对**你的生活**满意**吗？Dào mùqián wéizhǐ, nǐ duì nǐ de shēnghuó mǎnyì ma?

My family were **delighted/satisfied with** my artwork.

我的家人**对**我的作品**满意**。Wǒ de jiārén duì wǒ de zuòpǐn mǎnyì.

I never get **bored with** computer games.

我从不**厌烦**电脑游戏。Wǒ cóngbù yànfán diànnǎo yóuxì.

Adjective + about:

She is always **excited about** summer holidays.

她**对**暑假总是感到很**兴奋**。Tā duì shǔjià zǒngshì gǎndào hěn xīngfèn.

I am **not happy about** my personal life.

我**对**我的个人生活感到**不高兴**。Wǒ duì wǒ de gèrén shēnghuó gǎndào bù gāoxìng.

He was slightly **nervous about** his first day at school.

他**对**上学的第一天感到有一点**紧张**。Tā duì shàngxué de dì yī tiān gǎndào yǒu yī diǎn jǐnzhāng.

Adjective + from/for:

The book is **different from** the movie. 这本书和电影**不一样**。Zhè běn shū hé diànyǐng bù yīyàng.

I am not **responsible for** your health. 我不**对**你的健康**负责**。Wǒ bú duì nǐ de jiànkāng fùzé.

He is **famous for** TV ads. 他以电视广告出名。Tā yǐ diànshì guǎnggào chūmíng. (以 means 'for')

Adjective + at:

I am **surprised at/by** the prices.

我**对**价格感到**惊讶**。Wǒ duì jiàgé gǎndào jīngyà.

My daughter was **upset at/by** the terrible weather.

我女儿**对**糟糕的天气感到**不安**。Wǒ nǚ'ér duì zāogāo de tiānqì gǎndào bùān.

Adjective + by:

I was **impressed by/with** the of art at the National Gallery.

国家画廊的艺术**给我**留下**深刻的印象**。Guójiā huàláng de yìshù gěi wǒ liúxià shēnkè de yìnxiàng.

The audience were **shocked by** the blood in the movie.

观众**对**电影中的血腥感到**震惊**。Guānzhòng duì diànyǐng zhōng de xuèxīng gǎndào zhènjīng.

Adjective + of:

She is **tired of/sick of** looking after her younger cousin all the time.

她**厌倦了**一直照顾她的表兄弟。 Tā yànjuàn le yīzhí zhàogù tā de biǎo xiōngdì.

It was **nice of/kind of you** to help my son.

我**很高兴你**能帮了我儿子。Wǒ hěn gāoxìng nǐ néng bāng le wǒ érzi.

Adjective + of:

I am **afraid of** spiders.

我**害怕**蜘蛛。Wǒ hàipà zhīzhū.

My mother is **proud of me**.

我妈妈**为我**感到**骄傲**。Wǒ māma wèi wǒ gǎndào jiāoào.

The police are **suspicious of** our next-door neighbour.

警察**怀疑**我们隔壁的邻居。Jǐngchá huáiyí wǒmen gébì de línjū.

Adjective + at:

Are you **good at** sports?

你擅长运动吗？ Nǐ shàncháng yùndòng ma?

I am **hopeless at** all sports.

我对所有的运动都很绝望。 Wǒ duì suǒyǒu de yùndòng dōu hěn juéwàng.

Adjective + to:

Their kitchen is **similar to** ours.

他们的厨房跟我的很相似。 Tāmen de chúfáng gēn wǒ de hěn xiāngsì.

However, their dining room is **different to/from** ours.

然而，他们的客厅跟我们的不一样。 Ránér, tāmen de kètīng gēn wǒmen de bù yīyàng.

Adjective + with:

The city centre is **crowded with** foreign students.

市中心挤满了外国学生。 Shì zhōngxīn jǐ mǎn le wàiguó xuéshēng.

Adjective + in:

She is **interested in** contemporary art.

她对当代艺术很感兴趣。 Tā duì dāngdài yìshù hěn gǎn xìngqù.

He is **cultured in** a variety of languages.

他被培养(学习)各种语言。 Tā bèi péiyǎng (xuéxí) gè zhǒng yǔyán.

Adjective + on:

They have been **dependent on** their parents for years.

他们多年来一直依赖他们父母。 Tāmen duō nián lái yīzhí yīlài tāmen fùmǔ.

I am **keen on** gymnastics.

我热爱体操。 Wǒ rè'ài tǐcāo.

Noun + to:

I am responsible for the **damage to** the fence.

我**对**栅栏的**损坏**负责。Wǒ duì zhàlán de sǔnhuài fùzé.

I cannot understand his **attitude to/towards** his job.

我无法理解他**对待**工作的**态度**。Wǒ wúfǎ lǐjiě tā duìdài gōngzuò de tàidù.

There must be a **solution to** the problem.

这个问题必须有**一个解决方案**。Zhè gè wèntí bìxū yǒu yī gè jiějué fāng'àn.

Her **reaction to** his marriage proposal was amazing.

她**对**他求婚的**反应**是令人惊讶的。Tā duì tā qiúhūn de fǎnyìng shì lìngrén jīngyà de.

When I have time, I will send a **reply to** him.

我有空的时候，我会**回复**他。Wǒ yǒu kòng de shíhòu, wǒ huì huífù tā.

There are many **advantages to/in** travelling abroad.

出国旅行有很多**好处**。Chūguó lǚxíng yǒu hěn duō hǎochù.

Noun + for:

There was no **reason for** his quitting his job.

他没有**理由**辞职。Tā méi yǒu lǐyóu cízhí.

There has been a **demand for** more funding recently.

最近一直有增加资金的**需求**。Zuìjìn yīzhí yǒu zēngjiā zījīn de xūqiú.

I see **no need for** extra chairs in the dining room.

我认为餐厅里**不需要**许多的椅子。Wǒ rènwéi cāntīng lǐ bù xūyào xǔduō de yǐzi.

Noun + of:

Where can I buy a **map of** Britain?

我在哪里可以买到英国**地图**？Wǒ zài nǎlǐ kěyǐ mǎidào Yīngguó dìtú?

I have a **picture of** my family above the mantlepiece.

（我）在壁炉上面有一张我家人的**照片**。(Wǒ) zài bìlú shàngmiàn yǒu yī zhāng wǒjiā rén de

zhàopiàn.

Noun + of:

There is **a drawing of** Charles Darwin in that museum.

那个博物馆里有**一幅查尔斯·达尔文的画**。Nà gè bówùguǎn lǐ yǒu yī fú Chá'ěrsī·Dá'ěrwén de huà.

The **cause of** the fire is still unknown.

起火**原因**还不清楚。Qǐhuǒ yuányīn hái bù qīngchǔ.

The main advantage of playing sports is improved health.

运动的**主要好处**是改善健康。Yùndòng de zhǔyào hǎochù shì gǎishàn jiànkāng.

Noun + between:

What is the **difference between** a hurricane and a typhoon?

飓风**和**台风有什么**区别**？Jùfēng hé táifēng yǒu shénme qūbié?

There has never been a **connection between** the two of them.

他们**俩之间**从来没有**联系过**。Tāmen liǎ zhījiān cónglái méi yǒu liánxì guò.

Noun + in:

Throughout history there has always been an **increase in** population.

纵观历史，人口一直在**增加**。Zòngguān lìshǐ, rénkǒu yīzhí zài zēngjiā.

The company suffered a **decrease in** sales.

这家公司的销售额**下降**了。Zhè jiā gōngsī de xiāoshòu é xiàjiàng le.

Noun + with:

I often have **contact with** my other relatives.

我经常**和**我其他的亲戚有**联系**。Wǒ jīngcháng hé wǒ qítā de qīnqi yǒu liánxì.

An honest **relationship with** your boss can be beneficial.

与老板建立诚实**的关系**是有益的。Yǔ lǎobǎn jiànlì chéngshí de guānxì shì yǒuyì de.

I have some kind of **connection with** him.

我**和**他有某种**联系**。Wǒ hé tā yǒu mǒu zhǒng liánxì.

more and more (越来越), the more..., the more... (越..., 越...):

This place looks **more and more like** a modern house.

这个地方看起来**越来越像**一所现代化的房子。

Zhè gè dìfāng kànqǐlái yuè lái yuè xiàng yī suǒ xiàndài huà de fángzi.

He is playing football **more and more like** a professional these days.

如今，他踢足球**越来越像**一个职业球员。Rújīn, tā tī zúqiú yuè lái yuè xiàng yī gè zhíyè qiúyuán.

As time goes by, the **more and more comfortable** I feel living here.

随着时间的推移，我觉得生活在这里**越来越舒服**。

Suízhe shíjiān de tuīyí, wǒ juéde shēnghuó zài zhèlǐ yuè lái yuè shūfú.

Rodger said that his wife is becoming **more and more competent** with her new job.

罗杰说，她的妻子正在变得**越来越有能力**完成她的新工作。

Luōjié shuō, tā de qīzi zhèngzài biànde yuè lái yuè yǒu nénglì wánchéng tā de xīn gōngzuò.

The more you work **the more** money you get.

你工作的**越多**，你收获的钱**就越多**。Nǐ gōngzuò de yuè duō, nǐ shōuhuò de qián jiù yuè duō.

The more he practises **the better** he gets.

你练得**越多**会变得**越好**。Nǐ liàn de yuè duō huì biànde yuè hǎo.

The quicker you drive **the more dangerous** it is.

你开得**越快就越危险**。Nǐ kāi de yuè kuài jiù yuè wēixiǎn.

The slower you eat **the healthier** it is for you.

你吃得**越慢**，对你来说**就越健康**。Nǐ chī de yuè màn, duì nǐ lái shuō jiù yuè jiànkāng.

The higher the mountain **the bigger** than challenge.

山**越高**，挑战**就越大**。Shān yuè gāo, tiǎozhàn jiù yuè dà.

Unit 141

In contrast (..., 与此相反, ...) Conversely (反过来, ...)

on the other hand (一方面..., 另一方面)

Unit 142

尽管下雨，我们还是出去了。

除了你以外，在你家庭谁擅长运动？

Unit 143

把这件暖和的外套拿去，以防天气变冷。带一些额外的钱，以防万一你话太多了。

在紧急的情况下，请走楼梯。

Unit 144

我慢慢地开车，以便省燃料。我总是吃牛肉，好变得强壮。

为了成功，你必要进步。

Unit 145

我对他的行为很生气。她对暑假总是感到很兴奋。

我很高兴你能帮了我儿子。

Unit 146

这个问题必须有一个解决方案。

他没有理由辞职。飓风和台风有什么区别？

Unit 147

这个地方看起来越来越像一所现代化的房子。

你工作的越多，你收获的钱就越多。你吃得越慢，对你来说就越健康。

Index

Index

Index

Printed in the USA
CPSIA information can be obtained
at www.ICGtesting.com
LVHW082135111023
760666LV00012B/351